The Hanky of Pippin's Daughter

The Hanky of Pippin's Daughter

Rosmarie Waldrop

Station Hill

Published by Station Hill Press, Inc., Barrytown, NY 12507 with partial support from the National Endowment for the Arts and the New York State Council on the Arts.

Distributed by The Talman Company, 150 Fifth Avenue, New York, NY 10011.

Produced by the Institute for Publishing Arts (Open Studio Typography and Design Project), Barrytown, NY 12507, a not-for-profit, tax-exempt organization supported in part by the National Endowment for the Arts.

The Publisher gratefully acknowledges that extracts from this novel have been published in *The Newport Review* and *O.ARS*.

The author would like to thank the National Endowment for the Arts for a poetry fellowship which was partly used to work on this book.

Designed by Susan Quasha.

Library of Congress Cataloging-in-Publication Data

Waldrop, Rosmarie.
    The hanky of Pippin's daughter.

    I. Title.
PS3573.A4234H3   1986   813'.54   86-5919
ISBN 0-88268-038-2

Manufactured in the United States of America.

for Yerma

The Hanky of Pippin's Daughter

I

LAST SEASON'S BESTSELLER WAS *GREED*.

A useful word, you will find out. If mother had slept with Franz Huber (that was the name of the "mysterious lover," if you care to know, and I think you will: he may have been your father), if she had slept with Franz Huber out of greed it would clear the way. If out of vanity, as you think, it would still be simple: the accessories of the married woman. Consult any novel: she had to have her experiences. But in sex as in meteorology the number of particles in question is so enormous that an exact catalog of their positions and velocities is impossible.

How to get at their story? Do I even know their terms? A sarabande is a slow movement today, but it used to be a very fast dance. It's not a pretty story. No "credit" to the family. And that it took place in Germany is no excuse.

THEY GOT MARRIED IN JULY, 1926,

our father (maybe) and mother (always certain). Josef Seifert and Frederika Wolgamot. Already you complain: go farther back. But their courtship is your obsession, not mine. Nor do I know anything about it. Where I haven't a clue, surely I must shut up?

"On the contrary," says Bob, "you can tell it unmuddled by fact."

3

Bob. When he deigns to come out of his abstraction he is actually nosy. The other day I worked up the *Kinderszenen* again. Bob rushed out and bought Schumann's complete piano music. If it had been the *lieder* I wouldn't have been surprised. When there is a text Bob has an entry into the music. Too bad I'm not a singer. But piano music. Was he trying to show an interest in my work? Now? After all these years? Or was it a comment on my playing? I have still not come to terms with the Romantics, the music that knots your guts into a ball of vague but infinite desires. I do better where the strictness of the accompanying hand governs and sustains the impetuous flight of song. Clear lines. Transparent structure. My way into father's spiritual hierarchies? My way of being in a convent as you once were, Andrea?

MY HOME IS MY CASTLE,

our father quoted to himself. In English. But even castles have their back stairs which connect, always, with the zoo. How much more the ordinary home. This was his secret terror: that although nature makes jumps, man does not. So that his existence must deny the very principle (higher) by which he lives. That he must get down on all fours and draw out of his own body more links to the great chain of matter even while trembling with a lust for the ethereal, the subtle, the unapproachable mystery.

He stood at the window. The large summer sun was fading rapidly. The eye of Osiris. Violet shadows appeared along with a breeze. With all this weight, this monkey dance of matter, small wonder that the sun goes down. But that it should rise again and imprison time in the mystery of recurrence and the single instant. The "enormity" of life. Was he strong enough to free himself from the coils of the Ancient Serpent, to place his foot on its head and command its power, its blind force? Something in him distrusted his own will. His young wife agreed: a husband shouldn't have any will. Just when the sun touched the distant line of the woods, cut as if by a blade, Frederika called him.

"Right. Supper."

He stalled. Walked over to the barometer and tapped his finger against the glass. He was uneasy at meals. The reign of teeth, the too solid flesh. He dreamed of abstaining from meat, of a vegetable purity where the digestive process itself would pull him up into the light, a

4

brighter aura. And no more gas. But he loved his pork-chops, his leberwurst, his bratwurst, his currywurst. Reluctantly, Josef relaxed the effort to be pure. How ravenously Frederika devoured her food. Her whole being converged in her mouth. Teeth and lips worked their lethal caress. The throat stifled the shrieking pieces. He could almost see her turn, an unsated tiger, to spring on him. The meal finished, his knees trembled, but he was ready to throw himself on her. Fear swelled his tissues.

Frederika clattered with the dishes, mopped the table. A battle, and no quarter given by the wet cloth. When Josef put his arms around her from behind she braced her arms on the table:

"Everything at the proper time."

Pushed him off with her energetic rump.

SO WHAT COULD HE DO

but scratch his crotch and go to his charts where matter was rarefied in grids of curves and circles, helices, spirals, through its three stages of solid, liquid, gaseous, to approach the four states of Ether. Where the vital automatism of the body was the base for will and consciousness, which were the base for thought. Where the causal subsumed the spiritual subsumed the astral subsumed the electrical subsumed the chemical.

Where the dense body was enveloped by: the ethereal double,
ethereal double enveloped by: the ego body,
ego body enveloped by: astral body,
astral body enveloped by: mind body,
mind body enveloped by: causal body,
causal body enveloped by:
body of bliss.

Body of bliss.

Still, it must have been a summer of skin moist against skin. Heat rising. Light splashed against burning cheeks, eyes rolled back, shells straining to break, the force of a groundswell stirring the depth. Amoebas splitting, aping the contradictions of nature.

Josef's prick sailed toward a pale pink sunset, but he wondered why Frederika's saliva seemed more acid, her armpits saltier than his own. Repetition failed to do away with time, with self. As he plummeted he felt his soul as if it were a pain in his side. The weight of an ocean pressed on his spine. He toiled himself weary till a leaden dark grew behind his eyes and blacked out all astral flickers. Moments that hollowed the body yearning to lose itself in a deeper lust that would penetrate to the quick of the soul. It left him drained and unrefreshed, covered with sperm as with scales, when he would have grown wings.

He could not bring himself to talk about this. Still terrified, even with the blessing of church and state? Of thoughts that might become too definite if put into words? Did he sense disaster: a trace of impatience? A stillness beyond what the manuals knew of female passivity? A stiffening? Choppiness? Tides of refusal? He nailed her, but afterwards his soft member crept off her thigh and lay down in her disdain. Second thoughts or else the beginning of blind proceeding? When warm, saturated air blows over a cold surface, such as a cold current at sea or an icefield, the cooling may produce dense fog. It's only afterwards he finds out something has happened.

YOU CAN'T SAY

I didn't jump right in. With latitude, prevailing winds, and distribution of land and sea. First thesis: sex with Josef gave Frederika the impression that it was raining a lot outside. Logical enough when a woman takes a lover a couple of months after her wedding. You don't consider this. Because you, Andrea, want to damn her, the wicked witch who killed father, who sucked the marrow out of his will. The witch with the white gloves. With her eye on the clock. You think she married Josef because she was thirty, and the candybox half empty. A Herr Professor. Did it make up for his being a head shorter than she? Married him as a base of operation, a post from which to conquer the land, a fortress from which to make forays. Farther and farther into the field of friends, colleagues, new arrivals. Tomorrow the world. It only took her as long as two months because school was out.

The other teachers were on vacation. Our parents were not on a honeymoon trip. There was no money. Just to pay the installments on the furniture. Not to catch the globe in a net of latitudes and longitudes. It galled Frederika. She would have liked to write to her old friends in Berlin. Postcards from Italy. Greece. Paris. She had no desire to write them from Bayreuth. Bayreuth!

A town of Bavaria, Germany. 58 miles by rail N.N.E. from Nuremberg. Pop. 29,384. A railroad junction with an active trade, chiefly in grain and horses. It manufactures woollen, linen and cotton goods, leather, delft and other earthenware, and tobacco, and has also several breweries and distilleries. In Richard-Wagner-Strasse is Wagner's house with his grave in the garden.

SO WHAT DID THE NEWLYWEDS DO IN BAYREUTH, IN JULY, IN 1926?

Make love. At the proper times. Set up house. The four walls. The cell. The castle of refuge. The fortress to make forays from. What else? Like "cloud" or "temperature," no particular physical situation, but a distribution of possibles: Visit the Bayreuth castles? Galleries bored mother. But she felt at home in palaces, large spaces that belie their enclosure. Her mouth relaxed the moment she put her gloved hand on the gate of the Hermitage. Her small, soft, gloved hand. She forgot to look at the clock. She took possession. Sat down at the table, a Margravin rebuking her liveried servants. Decided on peace or war with the House of Ansbach in the conference room. She admired the terraces, the walls of the Orangerie. They were incrusted with iridescent shells to make up for the puny orange shrubs clinging to them, desperate in their search for warmth. She sat in the garden waiting for the carriages to draw up with galloping horses and coachmen in top hats cracking their whips.

Josef too liked the old grandeur. Spent weeks poring over maps, guides and artbooks to plan our summer trips. On the motorcycle. Him and me. Twenty years later. But he liked it with a grudge. He couldn't help translating the splendor into corvees, produce exacted from the peasants, extra taxes levied on the already poor, men called from the fields at harvest time to polish the ballroom floor. If he pictured himself in these surroundings it was as a servant. In regard to privilege (even of another century) he was as certain of being unqualified as I am when I watch a circus artist catch her trapeze between the hollow of one knee and the instep of the other foot.

As soon as we started up some palace steps a bit of a stoop came to his shoulders, the merest hint of submission. And a pull in his good leg made his step from one object to the next a little more syncopated, a little more nervous than it need have been, as if he were only sneaking a look, as if at any moment a bell could summon him to his duties.

Possible situations. Partial clues. On the hill, the Richard Wagner Festspielhaus wavered in the glare like Brünhild's rock when the ring of fire closes in on it. But here, at the edge of the pine dusk where Josef lay on his back in a thick smell of moss and wild lilac, it was—no, not cool. But compared to the heavy white heat... Josef loved to feel the earth press against his body, the little bumps and hollows resisting, uneven against his bones. Soil. Touching the ground. And to look up at the lacy branches shot through with sun. Sun and soil. Spirit and earth. Male and female. For this mother, the earth, he might accept the theory his friend Franz kept spouting. The Oedipus complex. Seeding the furrow that had formed him. No. An Antaeus complex would suit him better. Seeding for a race of giants.

He turned to look at the beautiful creature by his side. Her swelling softness. The sun caught in her curls. It seemed to him that he drew a richer, deeper intoxication from the shimmering blaze and fleshy green than ever before. The enormity of life. Of Nature. Of woman. Woman *was* nature. You can lay your hand on the bark, you can lie on the ground and imagine you feel the sap. But what is that compared to the—

"... unsanitary."

"What?"

"Chewing grass."

The blade was between his lips. He smiled because it suddenly took him back home, to the farm. He ought to jump up. The cows must be getting into the wheat. Or the onions. That would ruin their milk for a week.

Mother looked at her watch.

"I'm hot. And there isn't even a bench."

She was leaning against a trunk. A moment ago, Josef would have rhapsodized her flesh wedded to the tree in something like desire. But now he saw her lips pressed tightly together, the strained expression in her face, noticed her fidgeting.

"If you're uncomfortable let's go back home."

"But not through that wilderness."

Her voice was cross. As it had been on that "wretched path," his favorite shortcut across a tangle of grasses, weeds, burdocks, a wild profusion of purple thistles, all thick with the screams of crickets. He loved this time of the year, the overripe exuberance, the swelling plant flesh. And then the quieter pines, their copper glow, the heady smell of mint and heather.

"It'll be hotter to walk across the fields and down to the road."

"I don't care. I don't want another tear in my dress. You're too stingy to buy me a new one."

Bob always claims that any condition opens multiple pathways. But in Germany, I should say, some of those roads tend to be blocked. A soundboard, too, should respond uniformly to all the vibration frequencies in the range of the piano. But it's a matter of trial and error, the accoustical basis not well established.

WALKS THROUGH TOWN

were more successful. Houses lined up in rows. Streets, curving perhaps, but bordered, neatly divided into street and sidewalk, with the gutter between for proper drainage. Lines forming squares and circles. Mother's kind of space. And you could meet people, rummage through stores, pause at windows. Then she was content to take a turn in the shady Stadtpark. Mother had nothing against nature as long as it grew the proper paths and benches.

You got that from her, Andrea. Remember how Bob was alarmed when you insisted, last year, when we visited you in Munich, that we had to see some NATURE. He immediately saw himself lost in a wilderness, stumbling over roots, threatened by wild boars. But *your* idea of nature was the Amalienburg with its French garden, cone-shaped trees, square bushes, flower borders which form the letters: A M A L I A, a geometric display that subjugates fertility into a balance of pure form. Bob was relieved. He, too, prefers the human presence and its monuments, even if it means heaps of garbage. He would not, like the Indians, smooth out the sand over the place of his fire. But then, he wouldn't build a fire in the first place. And he doesn't pretend to love nature. Which is harder for us. Not love nature! Those years of indoctrination by father. But it took only with Doria, your twin, our quiet sister. Hikes through the woods any free moment she finds. Climbs mountains and hills where the air becomes blue memory of water folding her under. There she can walk without holding onto her balancing rod, husband on one side, five kids on the other, without watching the tightrope beneath her. She can stretch without encountering the durable grey of a wall. Her breath comes heavy, in handfuls. Nobody walks through it here. No husband. No children. Even when they are with her. Open space. Lengthening like summer days.

Leaving the park, Josef and Frederika found themselves in front of the square box of the "Bali Cinema." It cast a large shadow. Its slate roof seemed to exhale coolness, unlike the thick red tiles on the surrounding houses. Josef and Frederika lingered at the display cases. RASKOLNIKOFF leaned diagonally out of the poster.

"How about the movie tonight?" Josef suggested.

"I've seen it. A year ago. In Berlin."

HOW AM I TO KNOW

what belongs here and what should be left out. Or only waited for, surmised. A set of initial conditions from which something may follow. The solar constant before the influences of atmosphere and receiving surface. The themes of a fugue.

Andrea, you never consider that mother could have loved either Josef or Franz. Or at least desired. I admit the tone is not right. All that seemed to break through her icy armor were bursts of fury and smashing dishes. Hectic upbeats like the beginning of the *Kreisleriana,* syncopated lines and ghostly flitting dotted rythms. Volcanic eruptions whose ashes cut off the sun for long periods. Sensual? Only with food—and that had to be wolfed down by the clock. It's hard not to agree with your: "She had no use for sex, only for the power it gave her." But maybe at the beginning she thought more of sex. The penis in particular.

A REMARKABLE PIECE OF APPARATUS

which conjured up assemblages of valves, weights and counterweights, shafts, pistons, pipes, levers, screws, tubes, plugs. All streamlined and covered in the most modern and yet organic manner. Only the magnetic needle visible, rising to its true north undistracted by fur or measure or lip service from exploring the interior.

If the workings of the machine were vague to Frederika, something like the winding of a clock, a key entering the ignition, she had clear and precise ideas about its function and purpose:

1. Hoisting the subject (hydraulic lift? aerostat? balloon? airplane? wings? no matter) from the wintry regions of waiting to an everlasting blue sky.

2. Relocating the subject horizontally from paid-up marginal position to sun center with orbiting satellite(s).

3. Reducing the vast distance between wish and satisfaction to the merest rim of froth.

4. Absorbing the surrounding darkness which seemed to gather and flow from the empty space inside her.

In short: an express ride to the sun and moon of

FULFILLMENT

which she had been promised ever since she was a little girl. Fulfillment: all the myths spoke of it. The beginning of Everything out of Nothing, out of the yawning void of Ginnungagap which fire would drive from fog. The flaming sword would plunge into the icy rapids roaring down from the north, and a race of Gods would grow from her armpits. They would rule heaven and earth till the time when Valhalla would go up in smoke.

Josef, who was a head shorter than she and wore his hair parted in the middle, in a "popo part," Josef Seifert, 32, bachelor, the bringer of fulfillment? Of all the ways in which a woman can desire a man, I think our mother desired him thus abstractly. Like a sky without depth, without mass. As an appendage which had gone astray and was now restored to the rightful owner. Though I also wonder with you if she didn't simply desire A Husband and found it puzzling that Her Husband came with so many unnecessary back packs, salt tablets and astral doubles.

"Yes, I understand. You need a man," she said to me later. In Kitzingen. On the balcony that looked out on the Schwanberg. "But you don't have to go to America for that. We'll find someone here."

The mountain seemed blue and near enough to identify the castle where Pippin's daughter dropped her hanky, the one action out of her whole life I know about because it led to the founding of my home town, Kitzingen. Soon the Schwanberg would turn grey with the fall fog and seem as remote as the sun which I knew we would not get to see for months, though it would be hanging somewhere behind the watery curtain.

"You don't understand, mother. I want *this* man. Bob Harris."

The possession of a husband proved disappointing. It was not just that Josef was short: for lack of an orgasm the whole sky was empty for Frederika who anxiously sought this signal of a new era, a brighter galaxy of suns which would make the old one dim like a thing seen through somebody else's memory—her parents', for example, whom she never talked about except to complain that her father refused her voice lessons.

Mother was not given to blaming herself. While Josef rowed on into his sunset (albeit with the hope of a more ethereal dawn), Frederika had already gotten off the boat. Always precise in her timing, she decided to wait another four weeks. Come September she was ready for a different sailor.

As we know and Josef for a while did not: she got him.

SO WHAT THEY REALLY DID WAS:
WAIT FOR FRANZ

with the intensity of a slow introduction surging toward the allegro theme.

"My best friend," Josef said, stirring his lemonade, and perhaps added: "He's Jewish, but he is alright. Full of jokes. You'll like him. And he'll sing with you. He likes to sing. He sang even in the plane though the wind was taking our breath away."

"In the plane?"

"I've told you about it. Those double-deckers. Roland CIIs. Open. In the war. And I've told you about him: my co-pilot on most of the missions. All through 1915. 1916. Till we were shot down. We made bets which songs would bring luck. Not that I could hear them anyway, with the motor roaring and the wind. Once, when we had shot down three British planes, he shook his head: 'I sang them *God Save the King*, and instead of getting up they went down.' That's Franz for you."

Josef walked over to the barometer and tapped his finger against it. The needle quivered. A light breeze was coming in through the window. Wotan's breath. With a smell of hay. Of dust, too. The early moon changed shape from cloud to cloud. Thin ones. Like smoked glass.

"Flying... You can't imagine what that is like. Rushing into the air. Reversing gravity. Levitation. Up and up. Alone there with the clouds. In a grey fog. And if you lost connection with the ground—yes, it happened—then you were really alone. Just air, the immense, cold air. Unmapped. You could travel forever. A loneliness beyond any-

12

thing you can imagine, there, between earth and sky. A strange lightness. Brings home to you that there are other kinds of bodies than the physical, and thinner media than air.

"This Franz. Is he handsome?"

"And then searchlights. Flak. Let's hope they don't take me for a Tommy. Nerves tense to bursting. I navigate half by the instruments, half by instinct. There: the enemy machine in my cross. A 'Shark Mouth.' The hunt is on. I've got to get him. Fire. Comes at me baring his teeth. Lethal behind the paint. I pull the machine up to get around him. Flames. Smoke. I've hit him. But I can't hear the explosion. Eerie. Like a movie. Unreal. A wing bends, tears off flashing its red-white-blue circle mark. Hard to believe I've done it."

I bet, Andrea, that he didn't go on to tell mother how this feeling of unreality passed into a blind lust to shoot without even a care for his own safety. How he seemed already out of the battle, out of the body. Nothing could happen to him anymore. Nothing mattered but shooting, emptying the magazine.

"They want you to feel that way," Laff said to me. "Trigger-happy. That's why they train you like a circus horse."

Laff is *our* best friend, Andrea. The one you were supposed to pick up at the airport last summer, before he changed his plans. The one I said you'd recognize by the piece of pastry in each hand instead of luggage. Lafayette Pershing. He was in the air force too. The American air force. During the Korean War.

"Remember I've told you about the time we were shot down," Josef went on, absent-mindedly scratching his crotch. "September 20, 1916. Battle of the Somme. I'll have to show you the place on the map. Between Montdidier and Breteuil. Again I don't hear anything. Just feel the blow. Nothing. The rushing air. A maelstrom, mad spiral sucking me down. Then a sudden jerk: the parachute. I still don't know how Franz had unbelted and pulled me out with him. And how the parachutes opened without getting tangled. Down toward the towers of smoke beneath. Saved my life. And just said 'piffle paffle' when I tried to thank him."

"I'm getting another lemonade. Does he play the piano?"

"And then the transfusion. Group A, both of us. Blood brothers."

"No, I mean, does your Franz play the piano? You know I can't accompany myself."

But first, before Franz got back,

THE RING OF THE NIBELUNG

came round. Josef was an extra in Mime's smithy and had tickets for all four operas. For the first night Frederika chose a smart, fringed sheath, "provocatively chic." She was delighted to have it nearly peeled off her body by the expert eyes of the Bayreùthers who lined the approach to the Festspielhaus.

The Festspielhaus itself disappointed her. A big barn. No chandeliers glistening against red velvet. No splendor. No deep seats to sink into along with the waves of music. Wicker. Not even any arm rests. How differently things were done in Berlin. This would not impress anybody. No. It would have to be the "distinguished international audience" she would write about.

The music bored her. Hurrah for mother.

What have I done to be always surrounded by Wagnerians? Father first, you, Doria, and now Bob. I wonder, though, when you and Doria started making the pilgrimage to Bayreuth: were you not really in search of your infancy rather than of Lohengrin or Parsifal? Only, you overshot the mark, back beyond mother's womb into the empty air frantic to vibrate into a *leitmotif.* I am with mother here. Wagner is another murky mystery that eludes me. Just as I had no appetite for your religion, let alone your convent. Don't jump at the "your." I know, I know, I am talking about the past again, picking at your scabs. But is it the past? The violence of your reaction. The suddenness of your "conversion to dolce vita." Like mother, always to extremes.

Anyway, here I am with Bob, who also adores this wretched music, or, rather, I suspect, its dramatic, its literary side. We have made a pact that he will play Wagner only when I am out. I take care not to be back before four hours are over. Added advantage now: I don't risk finding him in bed with Gillian.

So hurrah for mother. She didn't like anything. The singers were fat. Crude statues with strained faces showing the pain this music causes to all involved. There was no action on stage. Not even the following nights when the story was supposed to get going, instead of three hefty Rhine maidens pretending to be afloat. Though, of course, it took a great deal of action and machinery to suspend the force of gravity, to make them seem weightless, like sails without a ship swaying in the painted waves. A labor betrayed only occasionally by an anxious glance at the dark space that unfurled below them. Were the ropes strong enough to hold both body and voice? During *Siegfried* mother also felt uncomfortably incomplete without her escort, even if he was a head shorter. That Josef was somewhere down in the orchestra pit, under that huge hood, one of the twenty extras who beat the anvils, one of the two hundred men making this deafening noise, no, it was no compensation.

"The singers are so fat! That Brünhild!"

Fat! Fat! You only see the outside. Brünhild's inner movement from the spirit world to the human is—"

"Fine spirit. More like a poster pillar. Your Siegfried too."

"Don't you see the grandeur of it, the *Gesamtkunstwerk:* drama, music, spectacle, poetry, myth, philosophy, wisdom—"

"All that fuss about a sword."

"But the meaning embodied in it! But the symbolism! The sword is the god-given substance. Remember, it was Wotan thrust it into the tree. But Siegfried, Man, needs to change it, file down the pieces and weld them anew to possess them as his own. To create his own identity. His own sword. Then he can do what Mime, the merely intelligent, merely clever man cannot do: slay the dragon of greed, Fafner, who sits on his gold, who only sleeps and owns."

"I wouldn't mind doing either one right now," yawned Frederika.

DAMN RIGHT I'M STALLING.

You go ahead, Andrea. You get mother's lover into this. You took the easy way out: "She was unfaithful. And in the first year of their marriage." All indignation and no particulars. A flick of the wrist. Your usual style. It was quick alright. "Most wicked speed," Josef quoted later. But that was the way mother ate.

It irritated Josef. Her plate empty when he had barely begun. The locust. As if she hadn't eaten for days—or a whole hour. Crunched away at the bone. Eager to get every little fibre of meat. How greedily her lips hugged her glass. He ate slowly. A bit like a horse, his upper lip pushed forward. He talked. Strayed from the task at hand. Her spoon played gavel:

"The soup's getting cold."

Called him back to the web where everything that could possibly exist started in her kitchen or armpit. A line of creation which does not run straight into the morning, but knots and curves back to the tonic, always.

Josef took revenge by telling stories of her greediness. How he wanted to introduce her to someone at a party, and her mouth was so full she couldn't answer for five minutes.

But as for greed, I remember their ritual to start dinner.

1. Josef looks at mother's plate: "Your chop is larger."
2. Mother's mouth tightens.
3. She trades plates. With a bang.

We play a comic variant of this. Laff with the girth worthy of his pastry consumption is always outraged at meals because Bob eats as much as he does and yet stays skinny. You must admit this is unfair to Laff who so loves to eat. Who, with all his dieting, always encounters a fatal pizza which has two more in its train. Who dreams of a slim body whenever he doesn't dream of Hollandaise, Béarnaise, Mornay, Velouté, Maltaise, Remoulade. Conflict stays his hand: the immediate pain of foregoing the dollop of cream, the delicate cookie, the delicious liqueur. Or the pang of conscience that catches up with him in his kidney. A stone, yes, which the doctor refuses to operate.

"With this layer of fat? Nobody can cut through that."

Complications. He reads books on dieting and feels he has done his duty.

"A pint of heavy cream, please."

"Try medium," says the dairy man.

"Fap. It's not the same."

"It whips. What's the difference?"

"It's not as heavy."

He puts the cookbook aside and reaches for *The Slimmers Who Stayed Slim*. Forty interviews. Miserable lives ruled forever by the calorie chart. Hovering over the scales and squawking with hunger. Dilated eyes at mention of food. Depressed by the endless struggle against the expanding universe.

No wonder Bob's appetite rankles him.

"Have you noticed, when we eat out, Bob always gets a larger portion?"

"Nonsense," I laugh at him. "Your eyes are larger than even *your* stomach."

That evening all three of us ordered roast veal at Guido's. The waiter served me and Laff. My portion was slightly larger. Laff got excited. Sat very still. Spun a coin in his mind and waited for heads or tails to round his proof. The waiter arrived with Bob's plate. It held two slices, each nearly as large as Laff's.

"You see?!"

"Nonsense. The portions are exactly the same."

OK. OK. I'll get to it:

INTRODUCING A LOVER, A SECOND THEME.

One afternoon, Frederika woke from a short nap. It was warm for September, damp with rain. But the wind had swept the smell of cabbage out and brought a trace of rotting fruit. She felt rested, light, and decided to sing which she had not done much lately. Why not? Possibly the piano was out of tune. Possibly Josef had a way of rustling his paper or going out for a walk whenever she sat down at the piano. But today, even before she got to the instrument, she had begun Orpheus's lament: *Ach, ich habe sie verloren.* E-major, the most beautiful key in the world. No other makes the notes rise like clear flames out of a limpid pool, makes them dance, their feet still moist, till the space grows beyond day or night, beyond death. Orpheus of the clear voice, of the golden lyre, the strong eye, the invincible love. Frederika pictured herself as both Orpheus and, a little ways off, Eurydice. In half-profile. The way she had posed for her photo in her new white dress. Her Eurydice in half-profile was just reaching out toward her front-view Orpheus when they came in.

Franz and Josef, "the late emperor," as their colleagues called them together.

"Wait till you meet Franz," Frederika remembered. "He'll sing with you. He teaches music. He once saved my life."

Franz Huber must be about thirty also. Not your conventional Orpheus: fat. Double-cone shape. With the icecream overflowing in the middle, just where you'd expect it. A round face, flushed pink, but with a marked chin. Auburn hair, curly. His clothes have a certain dash in spite of his shape. His gestures are bubbly: energetic tritones, leaping sevenths and double dots. Graceful.

I see him lifting his right hand, the thumb nearly touching the ring finger, trying to convey a subtle, elusive point. He looks like the angel in Crivelli's Annunciation. His fingers move with the small, precise motions needed for playing the piano or hooking the Holy Ghost to an eardrum.

Most important: full, sensuous lips which startled mother's hand. The small, soft hand she was so proud of.

"Nearly indecent, so soft," my friend Herman said later. "It leaves a pink blur in the mind."

Mother flirted with all my boyfriends. Shamelessly, I thought. With Herman more than with any other. The way she put her arm around his shoulders when she filled his cup, those ambiguous looks she shot back from the door. All the while lecturing me not to trust men in general and Herman in particular.

Franz ran to the piano and had her sing the aria all over again. Then the Schubert she knew. Then some Mozart. Then some popular songs. He taught her: "Yes, we have no bananas." The newest, he said. Sweeping the world from San Francisco all the way to Egypt. At least that part of the world which owned radios. He gleefully pointed out a little motif stolen from the "Hallelujah Chorus" and another from "Aunt Dinah's Quilting Party." Then, over coffee and, alas, no *Kuchen* (if Frederika had only known) he was a little disappointed that she had not seen the premiere of *Wozzeck*, last year, in Berlin.

THIS WON'T DO.

There was no photo. Not a ghost of a clue about Franz Huber. I looked through the albums examining every male. I looked for loose pictures, for places where pictures had been removed. Nothing. Nothing before you, the kids, the twins. Franz Huber is not only not there, but his absence is unmarked. No letters. Only one reference. When father found out about the affair, he consulted an oracle: Doctor Glahn, "Psychological Physician, Graphologist and Astrologer." Consulted him with photos of Franz and Frederika plus their birthdates.

I have Glahn's reply. An impressive letterhead where an eye within a triangle balances on the top of a caduceus, rays shooting sunlike in all directions. Glahn was cautious. But he gave Josef enough of what he wanted, to judge by the red underlining. This is where I got the sensual mouth, the marked chin "expressing willpower." Franz Huber's other traits are on loan from my friend (OK: lover) Laff. Mirror image. But listen: "A look of great intensity that could have near-hypnotic effect." Underlined by Josef. Of Frederika: "impulsive nature, sensual, weak-willed." The last should have made Josef laugh. But it gave him an acceptable version: "Frailty, thy name is woman." Frederika, not strong enough to resist the force of her own sensuality, let alone Franz's near-hypnotic powers? This cancelled out the first, worse possibility Josef had seen, his mind racing back and forth over his memories, and at the same time paralyzed, prostrate under the downpour, the *Landregen* that would not let up for weeks.

Franz Huber cannot be in the story. Yet he must. There is nothing that makes him visible. Least of all his hypnotic eyes. And his nose, though important, does not become fatal until some years later. It is only 1926.

I would like sentences that describe him as this void in memory, the photo removed without trace, the man whose name is never mentioned. As later, when I am a child, the word Jew is never mentioned. Except in Biblical history, by Father Ramberg. So that my Jews were, like the ancient Greeks, a remote people, striding with long beards and flowing robes through the *Nazarener* illustrations of my Bible. While the real Jews of Germany were herded through Dachau and Buchenwald and Belsen, expressway to death. Franz Huber most likely among them. Most likely already more deeply obliterated than by the Seifert family.

Now it seems peculiar to me that the Bible was taught at all in a German school, in 1943 or 1944. Side by side with Wotan defeating the Midgarth snake, the Niflheim giants kidnapping Freia and demanding her weight in gold. Greedy. We know where it got them. The last little chink had to be filled by the ring of the Nibelung. And a curse just will not be contained in a chink: the twilight of the gods. Valhalla goes up in smoke. As the Jews do. As Berlin does. And much of Germany. Of England. Of Poland. Of Belgium. Of France.

POSSIBLY,

Frederika took it as an omen that Gluck's name was misspelled "Glück" on the street behind the Paris Opera. Franz had told her, laughing at the French who seemed to think anything German must have its *umlaut*. Possibly she mused on the luck, the happiness of having this man appear who appreciated music—and had been to Paris. Possibly, thus lost in thought, she started in on the lost Eurydice for possibly the fifth time. Because the notes seemed to climb out of the underworld all by themselves, always for the first time, their virginity restored as by one of those fountains the goddesses know. Possibly it was then, on this same night, that Josef not only set his jaw, but said:

"Can't you stop this screeching."

Possibly he was exasperated at hearing the tune again and again. He did not have any virginal feeling about it. Or was there already a tinge of jealousy, possibly not even sexual, but because Franz had paid no attention to him? He had not gotten any chance to talk about the new tidal theory and how it might tie in with the Neptunism in the "Classical Walpurgisnacht" or with the Hwang Ho bursting its banks just last year. Or with the astral currents drawn by the Planetary spirits.

For whatever reason, he said it. If not this night, then another. A grinding dissonance. A deadly phrase which not only chilled mother to the bone, but settled in the marrow where it kept regenerating and spread frost through her whole body for at least forty years. Cold tends to persist. A stable equilibrium. When I get around to making a list of things mother used to say it will be number one in frequency, or number two, right after:

"That's *your* problem."

If Josef wanted to make love this night he encountered snowy peaks. If he fucked anything in the next several nights it was memory, though, as he was nothing like Zeus, there is no record of a birth of muses to ring his tail while he jacked off and jacked off until his final triumph over time. For you remember: the periods of refusal got longer and longer, till mother moved out of the bedroom altogether. I was put in her bed. This was in 1946. I was ten. And though I suppose all the earlier punishments ended with Josef's unconditional surrender—one does not bargain with Fredericus rex, with the king of Prussia—this last time he did not give in.

I pretended I was asleep when father came to bed, but watched, between half-closed lids, his furtive movements as he undressed and took his wooden leg off. Years. I don't remember how many. Watching, every night, for a glimpse of his penis slipping out of his shorts, from under his shirt, from the slit in his pajamas. Soft worm, coming out after the rain. Dozens of them. Hundreds. Guiltily I tried not to look, shut my eyes tight, turned over, put my head under the blanket. The room filled with them. Thousands, like schools of eels, swimming dark, purplish. The sea rose, swelling the brooks and rivers far into the land. Body next to body, they traversed the space, fish, arrows propelling themselves, I saw them. The water rising the whole time. I swam and swam. And there was father at the diving board. His penis crept out of his bathing trunks onto his left thigh. I dove, put my face under water, but I was awake. Here he was going up on the board again. Herman started to titter. This time I'd have to tell father.

Never after did a penis seem this large, not even in erection. Of course the houses seem smaller also, the leaning tower of Kitzingen a mere toy. The only eels I've seen in a long time were smoked and marinated, in small cubes of aspic.

But that was twenty years later. Now Josef suffered in spite of still having both his legs. The chilling of the ground especially sensitive at night. Got horny. His groin in waves of caressing pain. Unbearable. To have a wife and still not get it. He would have liked to roar his rage out like a bull. Or be ascetic enough to allow his soul to rise, to free itself from the fatal attraction, the blind force and fire: "Let me loose, O mother earth, that I may carry thy word to the stars." But his body held on with the memory of Frederika's touch on his skin like claws, soft claws, nearly indecent so soft. No way to escape into the world of purity, of concepts, of death and perfection. Naked thoughts. Indecent. Spreading their poison through him, weakening him. A brothel, a stinking brothel, and no satisfaction guaranteed.

No matter how he scrubbed his body, how much cold water he threw on it, how much he ran and exercised... How had it all happened? How could it happen like this? Impossible to clarify, to hold it in with a word like love or sex or even passion. A nightmare he felt in his belly, his balls, but which he did not understand, which he could not explain by any of his charts.

It took more than one try to mollify Frederika. Only her hand was soft. Day after day, snow radiated a thick silence.

DEAR ANDREA,

I'm taken aback by your: "Now it becomes clear why you are taking mother's side." Scandalized that I have a lover! As if you were still in your convent. You of all people. May I remind you of *your* affairs? May I quote a well-known rock song:

My favorite lover: a Carmelite nun
who converted to *dolce vita*.

Have I objected to your sleeping around? From what *you* told me it sounds like you take on every man you interview. Is it written into their contract that they get to sleep with you? Part of their fee? I'm sorry. I don't mean it. But I don't see what's so different. So you're not married to Antonio. But you are living with him. Of course he's only your sexual athlete, your *maestro d'amore* (isn't it funny you have to put this in Italian). And he doesn't read anything but comic strips and *fotostorie* which isn't up to madam's intellectual pretensions.

Cross this out. I'm sorry. But if you have needs that are not satisfied by one man, why can't I? Or are you still righting the balance of the universe? Once you prayed all day to make up for those who didn't. Do you now feel there is not enough sex, and you, Andrea Seifert, have to tip the scales all by yourself? Or is your ship caught in a hurricane, the second phase now, raging in the opposite direction? But still the same storm: madonna or whore, the Catholic image of woman?

And how can you help it when your initiation came kneeling at the feet of a priest, when the hand that had absolved you pushed your head into his lap, pushed his penis into your mouth like another communion wafer. You were frozen, you said, as his hand gripped the back of your neck and gently massaged it, pushing and pulling, making you move your head slowly, move, lick, slowly, suck. You gagged, you said, as he came, your stomach rising into your throat. And then both of you knelt together, prayed, asked forgiveness.

BUT YOU DON'T KNOW BOB.

You know—no, don't interrupt, I'm not saying you know only his social side. I think you know at least a little the Bob who is *the* face for me, *the* you, deep, silent, *the* hands, blood pulsing under thin membranes, open lips. Necessary as air, as a soundboard. He is written into my body. If he left I would dissipate, a faint noise hanging in the room.

But you do not know how uneasy he makes me all the same. It's not just that he is indifferent to my piano. Sometimes I feel there's too much of me for his taste. A trace of shrinking as my tongue pushes into his mouth. An impulse of flight, broken, as I rub my breasts against him. Even my words too tangible, almost solid in the air. My gestures seem to accumulate, build up a larger body around me. Buds opening out in all directions, curves exploding, wine spills and soaks the grass, the single note grows into a chord.

Bob's eyes cloud with anxiety. He gets off his chair, avoids brushing against my arm with a shadow's ease, his shoulders hunched, his arms held close to the body, always. Like Chopin at the piano. His pen. He clutches it when he has to talk as if he wanted to assert that writing comes before the voice. Covers small bits of paper. Index cards. One. Another. The importance of detail: Emily Dickinson's "slant of light." Clockwise movement in *The Sound and the Fury*. He sits at the window for an hour, looking out. Locked in his head, in his words which come out slowly, hesitantly.

"May I come in?" I ask.

"Oh. Why. Yes."

"Am I bothering you?"

"Yes. But, no, not if . . . "

"How is it coming?"

"Oh, slowly."

His eyes pulled, always, by something beyond my shoulder, behind my head. Even when he looks into my eyes he looks beyond. As if something he needs were hovering there, ready to come to him, but stopped by my too opaque shape. Sometimes I think I don't know him at all. Skins inside skins. Cavities inside cavities. Mirroring walls. A world as uninhabitable as father's astral spaces, even though the conjunctions are not of planets, but Lambert Strether hanging fire while Bartleby prefers not to.

Meanwhile he builds himself a cell within his study, a labyrinth of tables and shelves sufficient to disorient a demon. Walls within walls, silence within silence, monk's rectangle of chair and typewriter, safer and safer from me.

Laff is so much simpler. Maybe just more like me. A musician, for one thing. Tones going out into the air, breaking, thrown back, always perceptible and easy. The perfect playmate. Definite, clean lines.

"Clean" makes me laugh: Laff is a real American. A race as clean as the Germans, as mother, as a Mondrian line. You would like him. He's as scrubbed as you are, as eager to wash as Doria with her two baths a day. A scent of soap hovers about him always, of aftershave, of lotions. He navigates my body like a tub, too, whistling, filling the resonant spaces with his voice, his sex. All smooth as the smoothest *savon*.

At least, he does not whistle Wagner, thank heaven. This is a concession to me. With Bob he talks Wagner, listens to Wagner without end. But Laff's whistling is another matter.

"I like a tune you can whistle," Bob said to him.

"Piffle paffle. You don't like a tune *I* can whistle," said Laff and started in on Schoenberg's second quartet.

No complications, no uneasiness as with Bob. Though perhaps our moments of happiness, Bob's and mine, are more poignant for being laced with anxiety. A deeper pleasure. But yes, O my literal-minded sister, I can depend on coming with Laff. Which goes to show how wrong those ads and movies are which codify acceptable eroticism as between spare frames, the lean and hungry look, as father would quote. Though this was a point on which he disagreed with Caesar.

"You're eating too much, Frederika. You're getting fat. A fat body adds incalculable weight to your soul. Why do you think gluttony is a deadly sin?"

Not that Laff escapes fear of fat and hellfire. He too thinks of his paunch as a calamity, but because it lands him on the horns of not eating or self-destruction. How he longs for Germany with its cafés full of hefty consciences calmly consuming their cake *mit Schlag* (*heavy* cream, it goes without saying) and *doppelte Portion.* How he longs for the fleshy Victorian age whose very music moved in heavy, lush, sensuous masses of domestic bliss. Though even there, underneath, lurked a lust for the lean, the delicious contrast, the skinny and unsated, the frail modulation, hard and soft blurring in ambiguous tonality.

Forgive me, Andrea, if I *am* making a little fun of your cleanliness, your misery when you have to miss your shower or run out of soap. Names. Their signals. How could a Seifert do without *Seife.* How was that in the convent, by the way? Were you allowed to wash or was that another pleasure of the senses to be given up? So that the soul could be whiter, more resplendent than the skin? Pores clogged against the touch of air, against sensations the size of a pinprick? While the soul was treated with its own Mr. Klean. Scrubbed with confessions. Bright red for the sake of heaven. Scraped as deep as the lungs can reach.

AM I TAKING MOTHER'S SIDE?

Can I possibly isolate any one particular event as the cause of other particular events? Construct a different family myth out of one little sentence? A myth where the evil does not emanate from mother, the wicked witch and the cold void inside her, but from this little sentence? Father's "Can't you stop this screeching?" A Pandora's box of polar conditions, blizzards and ice-storms, all roads coated with the slippery, treacherous layer so that progress is precarious, accidents frequent, the total of broken limbs still not counted up.

under Frederika's feet. Just when it turned brown outside, when mallows signaled the beginning of autumn. Her ice broke. Her laughter bubbled up between the floes. Josef let himself glide into her fluidity even though it ran into scales and tunes. There was much singing that fall. Frederika studied Italian and French. She added *Plaisir d'amour* to her repertory, *Piangete, ohimè piangete* and *Un certo non sò ché*. She sang *J'ai perdu mon Eurydice* instead of *Ach, ich habe sie verloren*.

Josef walked over to the barometer. The needle pointed to Steady.

When Frederika did not sing there was the radio, bought on the installment plan. A peace offering. Though perhaps Josef's right hand took back what the left had given and knew about it too. He had resisted with diatribes against fads and gadgets until somebody, maybe Franz, tipped him off that the annual Wagner festival was scheduled to be broadcast. He could hear how it had sounded to the audience when he beat his anvil, rather than the deafening clang at the back of the orchestra, nearly inside the resonant iron, dark, sucking the rhythm down to the pit of his tight stomach while his arm went on beating all by itself. The radio was bought and, tonedeaf as he was, Josef developed a passion for opera. Witness the rows of "Reclam's Libretti" in his bookcase. All annotated in the texts and with lists of singers next to the arias—singers he must have heard on the radio. Programs stuck in where he had seen the opera. All of Wagner. *The Magic Flute*. A few others.

"You listened to all these singers, father. Why do you hate it when mother sings?"

Josef's eyes came back from some interior space into the net of deep furrows and still looked right past me. As Bob does now.

"It's not just her. Women shouldn't sing at all. Their voices are too high. Now Wagner, he knows this. He treats them recklessly, deforms them till they are something else. Not female, not male either, not voices really. Something like raw passion."

More like noise, I thought. You know I never could stand Wagner. Which is why I resent it doubly that you gave Bob the *Parsifal* for his birthday. That deafening murkiness, that fury from somewhere beyond crowding into my space. Though I ought to appreciate the economy of your little game: pleasing Bob and swatting me at the same time.

25

874941

Meanwhile, Josef had gone on about concave magnetism and into a full-blown description of mother's voice.

THE VOCAL TISSUE OF FREDERIKA SEIFERT, THE SINGER:

Tone color: a central brown radiates from the vértical axis like a mandala in honor of motherhood which has replaced virginity, the color of the invisible, as said Couperin. A spot of shrill pink appears, however, on the vowel "i" and shades toward black as Orpheus step by step loses his Eurydice.

Texture: a throaty gouache with a vaginal suggestion of watered silk.

Line: sharply rising on strong emotion from trembling tremolos to the jagged heights of an encephalogram.

Timbre: trees falling.

Ornaments: all the letters of the alphabet, a scale of melismatic sighs and groans, mordent quavers, sibilant somersaults.

Edges: rough. Torn, not cut.

By the time I paid attention to mother's voice it was, of course, much older. I agreed with father and wished she'd shut up.

FREDERIKA WAS PROUD

to have a lover. That first Monday. The last note of *Plaisir d'amour* had hung in the air. And faded. They looked at each other.

"The Pergolesi now?"

The silence did not give. It grew. It took Frederika into a different space. Like a park at night where the thick birches gleam even whiter in the moon, and the distance between bodies follows the law of the tides. The silence flooded. It had already undressed her before Franz got off the piano stool. The sound of her clothes was loud enough in her ears to alert the whole neighborhood. Franz's voice suddenly went a fifth higher. His alarm touched her first, before his hands. It made her body more yielding, stirred a motherly feeling into the challenge she had thrown down with her blouse. As he pressed her against his body his breath came hard, pulsing with sudden, quick, stifled laughs which would have startled her if she had not been too occupied with the way he played her skin from the hollow of the knee to the taut nipples.

"Frederika, Rikele, how could we."

"How could we not."

Now she let Franz undress her slowly, in front of the mirror. With delays and temporary diversions, the way a melody resists its inevitable goal. Watched his eyes grow dark against her whitening presence, tension contracting his pupils. Watched the trace of terror in them as she swung her breasts against his chest. So full. So much of them. Watched his throat contract with a desire too large for their bodies, but which homed in on her skin and burned it.

Not as with Josef where she felt stretched into the angles of a trapeze on which he swung, trying to take flight into the mirage of life-*an-sich*, of mysteries as far this side of penetration as beyond analysis.

ANDREA, ANDREA, ANDREA.

I'm sorry. Yes, it's different. I know it's not the same with Antonio and you. I apologize again for the "intellectual pretensions." You know I don't mean it. On the contrary. I'm puzzled that you don't get more bored with Antonio. It's restful to be with him, you say. No anxieties. (And you don't see why I want Laff?) This really is you. Out of the convent and into the arms of a man who looks at your body only. Looks. Rubs. Pokes. Pinches. Strokes. Sniffs. Whose German isn't good enough for an extended conversation. Who would probably be stupefied if you tried to tell him what goes on in your head. So you just press against him hard and tango around your living room to *O sole mio*. Maybe this is what you need after years of denying your body, of trimming it into a French garden. Still, always to extremes. Like mother.

In a way, Antonio has become your convent. Do you remember what you said was hardest? Not to talk. Your most frequent punishment the piece of wood tied over your mouth: BROKE THE RULE OF SILENCE. Only, Antonio is more successful than the nuns because the few things he can talk about, like food, don't count for you. Laff would be incensed: what more delightful topic than a *suprème de volaille Normande* smothered in mushrooms, the vermouth and cream bathing the delicate morsels. But this is not what you want. You need to run off to your celebrities. From the vow of silence to the radio. Always to extremes, as I said.

27

But I begin to see the advantage of silence when you get on the high horse: "How can you do this to Bob who worships the ground under your feet." You forget that he also worships the ground under Gillian's. No, Gillian was not a joke.

A cozy foursome, don't you think. Except that it is already over. All spring I've defended myself against the knowledge that Laff is leaving, straining to get away. Belly and prick erect, he ploughs into the uncertain air toward academic posts or orchestras. I have fought against the summer bounding in, crowding with fists, elbows, piffle paffle and auditions, with the arteries standing out on the temples and neck from the strain. All spring I've wanted just to throw myself down on my bed and pretend it was still winter. And stop it all. Not go on. Put my hands under my head and play dead. Idiot that I am, I have anticipated his leaving, lived his coming absence along with his presence. As if I had no sense of sequence, of time and measure, three four, four four, five or eleven against seven. Not one note after the other, but pressing the whole arm down on the keyboard as Laff likes to do. Layered sound, but massive, no cracks, no articulation.

WHAT DO YOU SUPPOSE THEY TALKED ABOUT, FRANZ AND FREDERIKA?

I don't think Franz talked about his childhood any more than she did. Not of his father's Yiddish newspapers folded around the racing sheets. Of his mother's brooches, her white face, or the declamatory leaps of synagogue music. Certainly not of silver candlesticks and the hopelessness of Jewish prayers. Nor of the blond Hans or Fritz who tripped him on the way to school and chaffed him when he kept his distance:
"Why don't you walk with me? Scared, Itzig?"
Possibly he told of his father:
"Franz, you got to face reality. Music is nice at a wedding. I don't say no. But the other days, how are you going to eat?"

Certainly Franz told of his

TRAVELS.

This was what Frederika wanted to hear. Travel broadens. Even just hearing about it. It adds whole countries to our inner dimension.

Spreads us over larger and larger areas until I have a toe stuck in Kitzingen am Main while my left earlobe touches San Francisco. Frederika did not want to hear about just any travel. Not about Josef's trips which were all hiking through woods or bicycling to some church or museum.

But Franz's travels were full of magical names. Piccadilly Circus. Regent Street. Place de la Concorde. Via Barberini. Rue du Dragon. Piazza di Spagna. Les Champs Elysées. Rue Pauline Borghese. Albert Hall. Le Louvre. Rue de l'Epée de Bois. Elephant and Castle. Names which she invested with the splendor of a fata morgana while thirsting in the desert. She would have believed in streets paved with opals, crystal palaces, temples of amethyst. And, though Franz had not likely been there: La Tour d'Argent, Le Lapérouse, Simpson's, The Walterspiel, The Ritz, The Claridge.

When this made them restless they went out for a walk. Franz did not lead her into the wilderness. He was content to stick to the streets and the park, to pause at a shop window or break a small twig of jasmine to tickle Frederika's nose. They stopped in at Café Wolf where the waiter in his crumpled tails wiped his hand before he held it out to Frederika:

"How are you today, Frau Professor."

"How are you, Herr Anton," she put her hand in his.

He seemed to hold on to it for a long time. So Franz said haughtily: "Garçon!"

Anton bowed, and when he brought their cognac and coffee and *torte* he did not make a single remark like:

"We need a strong government. In times like these... Now other countries... Pilsudski... Carmona... Mussolini."

Or even:

"If the mayor knew what he was doing. But a socialist. No sense of the true interests of the town."

He loved to talk politics. But now he was offended. "Garçon" indeed. He let his arm hang down limp like a fin.

Later, Franz and Frederika picked up Josef at school. Anton saw the three of them pass by again, and his hand got a little damper.

"Rikele, I feel bad about Josef."

"Let me tell you, you're doing him a favor."

"Fap. I didn't think you'd be so cynical."

"If it weren't for you I'd have left him by now."

Franz squealed with laughter. It shook his belly and made a little squeak when he inhaled:

"You mean I'm saving his marriage by giving him horns?"

"I don't see what's so funny."

ANDREA,

I did not mean to be flip about your leaving the convent. I realize it was more than a change of profession. How did you bear to stop being who you thought you were? How did the nuns convince you that you had only *played* dead? Acted a part which you had no talent for? Caught in the trap of life. After baring your skin and folding it back from your soul, preparing for the knife, preparing to be a victim to appease the wrath of god. I don't see how you could stand either, entering the Carmel or coming back out. Though I am glad you are back. But are you not still trying to do away with yourself? In sex, this time. In this act which is both intimate and the most impersonal? Do you still have a body left? Have you not lost it in the mirror gallery of the flesh which multiplies the body into sheer matter to the point where it curves into concept and is abolished: you and father join in a landscape of pure spirit? You and Josef, that is, who may not be your father. But if he did not give you any genes he still formed your mind, gave it a lasting dizziness the way he snatched you up from the floor where you might have gone on playing with dolls and toy casseroles. He swung you up toward some crystal chandelier of the spirit world, then, losing interest, bumped you down as suddenly, leaving you breathless, the doll dangling from your hand by a twisted arm or leg.

Franz and Frederika had gone to a concert while Josef stayed home. The wind had died down. A few drops of rain were still falling. Straight now, following their own weight without being driven off course and against the window. The force of that wind.

Josef tapped his finger against the barometer on his way to the window. The sky was dark, without a single reckless star. He thought he could detect a semblance of writing in the wet traces on the pane. If he could only read it. Traces. Footprints. Passage of spirits. Not to mention the large-scale message of the stars. He sat down with his charts and pendulum. Listened for some other voice to come to him. Sometimes, something seemed to come. It thrilled him. But he checked and rechecked, counted and recounted, afraid of twisting chance into authority.

Retreated into his inner ear and seemed impervious to what went on around him. Then the startled surfacing. Fear of drowning, of quicksand. "These experiments are fraught with danger." What would it be like to rend the veil? Like having the plane rise too fast? Mountain sickness? When the change of pressure is rapid the result may be fatal: Croce-Spinelli dead in his balloon, in 1875. *Der Mensch versuche die Götter nicht.* The sober dawn. He tried to take comfort from it. Shivering though the apartment was warm.

Then all three went to such dances and parties as there were. Christmas parties. New Year's balls.

"Hurrah for the *grossdeutsche* solution," they were greeted. "Prussia and Austria in harmony."

Josef was tickled to play the part, to form the late emperor's name with Franz. He had liked Franz Josef. The last of the old school, he said. And a tragic figure: his brother Maximilian in Mexico, the empress Elisabeth, the crown prince Rudolph. Violent deaths, all of them. And the end of the empire. Franz Josef. Names fascinated him. He wondered why Frederika refused to call him Josef. *Beppo,* she insisted. Short for Giuseppe. Placing him in a landscape too clear and sunny, of belcanto and castrati rather than webbed counterpoint. Names. Their signals from the past. *Fredericus rex, our king and lord,* we all sing later, ambiguous family hymn to mother, Frederika, our Prussian king. Trying to cover up terror in brisk, martial jocularity, masking the downward slide of courage as mere passage work and appoggiatura.

Frederika drew disdainful comparisons between these provincial balls or *tanztees* in Bayreuth and the thrill of the "Foxtrot-Casinos" on Kurfürstendamm. A Berlinerin does not easily adapt to small-town life. But she liked to dance. She must have been a hurricane when she allowed her gestures to break out. Usually they were reined in by force and fidgeted for a chance to get away. Like her three daughters.

MEANWHILE, 10 BLOCKS FROM THEIR APARTMENT,

there died, on January 9 of 1927, a dismal grey day, Houston Stewart Chamberlain. Author. Philosopher. Locally known best as Richard Wagner's son-in-law.

"Did you see the paper? The emperor sent a representative to the funeral."

"Good for the Kaiser. Well he might. A great philosopher. *The Foundations of the Nineteenth Century. Race and Personality. Race and the Nation.*

"You know who else was there?"

"Who?"

"Adolf Hitler."

"Who?"

"The putsch in Munich: Hitler and Ludendorf, a few years back, don't you remember?"

"Oh. Vaguely. There were so many. Isn't he supposed to be in prison?"

"He was right here in town."

"Make a speech?"

"I don't think they'd let him. After a putsch."

"Might have been interesting. Lots wrong with the government."

"It's not doing so badly now. Got rid of the inflation. Unemployment is down too."

WHAT A STRANGE CHALLENGE, ANDREA.

I have not *boasted* of Laff. It's playing, you say. I have not lived, you say, until I have lost myself. Degree zero of consciousness, the price of happiness. Because we only exist in the spark that passes between two beings, not in holding on to ourselves. Your wildness frightens me. We haven't gone far enough, you say, if we can go farther still. Something in me reels every time you open a door, whether it is the door of a church or a bedroom. Because you step into the region of the immoderate, of floods, of calamities. For as long as we have a body, Andrea, we can always go farther still. But is there no choice but ONE or a mob? Monotheism or a pagan Olympus?

As for Laff, I did not meet him singing Gluck, but playing the first Bartok concerto. One of the few times the New Music Ensemble ventured into orchestral dimensions. Laff was one of the additional winds. We got to talking in the rehearsals. He actually clarified my sense of the concerto, of the toccata-like structure of both the allegros. A marvelous musician. Everybody was happy he stayed with the Ensemble when it "slimmed down" again. Yes, we do make music together. He's even trying to help me with improvising. He gets out his clarinet, and I have to do my damnedest to keep up with his explosions. Screaming down the sky.

Anyway, I am not telling you my life while pretending to imagine mother's, though I am disturbed by their parallels. How did it happen then? My God, how does it ever happen. Sudden drop in the temperature. Or sudden rise. Nearness. His hand on my shoulder. My hand on his, accidentally, momentarily. From friendly to intimate. Flare-up. Abrupt chill. Unnerved by the thought of meeting him I spent hours by the phone starting to beg off from rehearsal, but putting the receiver back down before getting through. Then he moved into our attic. Sometimes, just passing him on the stairs I had to sit down on the steps and hold on to the bannister.

Acting like a teenager, you'll say. Exaggerating, striking louder chords than the score calls for. OK. But it shocked me out of the promise of routine. There it was again, the thump of the heart, the brief poison and feeling myself in every little gesture, even pouring a glass of wine.

Maybe it's simply a mechanism: you see a door and you go through it. Then the door may fall shut behind you. The game turns into mistake. With a fine of pain. Or into a bird's take-off into the deep of the air. With a fine of pain also. Pain seems to be the constant, no matter how we turn our words or bodies.

He didn't "seduce" me. Didn't have to. Not with that name. Having married Bob Harris, the plainest name in the world, how could I have resisted Lafayette Pershing! If anybody seduced, it was me. Like mother, but not like mother. Not like I think she did it, not like a challenge: either yes or the priest's knife and a team of raging horses. But now I get doubts again. This is mother as I knew her—but was she like this twenty years earlier? When she must have felt the ordinary kind of loneliness, of anger, of surprise? When she danced? Danced far into her

PREGNANCY.

She happily danced out of earshot of the spiteful comments:
"In her condition!"
"You don't suppose she's trying to lose it?"
On the contrary. Mother's happiness grew with her belly. No

morning sickness for her. She discovered large territories inside herself, full of exotic vegetation. Her chest expanded with a whirring hum as she devoured the air, the green hills of Bayreuth, and down to the stone of its houses to feed this interior continent, the pulsing rivers which circled the new island. The sun was a copper gong. Pods and berries spilled from the branches, a soft vegetable rain. A new world. And of her making.

"Frederika Seifert's pregnant. I saw her queuing at the butcher."

"By whom, do you suppose?"

"Ah, a most interesting case of necrophilia: the late Emperor."

"Maybe she'll have twins: one each."

"Come on, don't be nasty."

"Who's nasty?"

"Coming to the Schwaben Inn?"

"There's that talk tonight..."

"One of your liberals? Goody-goody-talk? Don't you know that human nature doesn't change? Struggle for survival, that's all."

"Yes. The Right of Young Nations. Expansion. The increasing birthrate. Evolutionary justice."

"Piffle paffle: the birthrate hasn't gone up in 30 years."

"You're just being contrary. A typical example: adrift, no spiritual moorings. Next you'll become a Marxist."

"We need ties, not dissolution."

"If Moeller van den Bruck were speaking I'd go: 'The Race of the Spirit.'"

"You're safe. He's joined that race."

"But don't you agree: we must save human nature from the machine."

"Is that what the talk's on?"

"No. 'Our National Revolution.'"

PREGNANCY.

A time full of itself. To the brim. Frederika hummed as she got up in the morning. Hummed as the sun slid its big belly over the rim of the horizon. Hummed while fixing breakfast. Hummed in the street, shopping. Hummed as she passed the policeman. He was sorry there was no traffic he could stop for her.

"When I met her she was like a jet of water bubbling up into the sky," said father, sadly.

Was it the pregnancy that weighed her down, made her join all the other bodies falling through the first person singular toward age and death? The dew-point where the moisture collects into drops? So that the airy jet that had floated up into the sky fell back in violent thunderstorms, torrential cold showers which beat father's face down to the whorls we knew.

And the hardness? An "I" freezing into hailstones in the rapid up and down drafts of motherhood, in the high tension of its stormclouds, the abnormal cold in the higher strata?

I remember how she stood on the little balcony, her lips pressed together, one fist stuck in her apron pocket, the other holding the alarm clock. Watched the sky darken, the red emptiness where the sun had been, watched me come home. If I seemed to dawdle I could sense her disapproval from a block away, her lips pressed tighter still.

PORTRAIT OF FREDERIKA AS A CONTROL TOWER:

A structure like a glacier, transparent from long-continued compression, rises on the field of an enormous clock. From a distance, nearly promising warmth, but with an air of determination strong enough to withstand the tension of 230 piano strings. No stairway, no window. All energy is concentrated at the top. A brilliant steel-blue light. One might have enjoyed it if it had brightened and warmed in accordance with need. A look of polished metal which, like the frog's eye, doesn't report the object, but only the object's movements. All its movements.

Then the sudden beam shoots down its barrel, pins inmates, conspirators, fugitives to the wall like insects. And just as suddenly goes out and leaves me in the dark, screwing me still tighter against the silence, a stabbing terror in my chest, a foreboding of the pleasure of flight and the volley of bullets that would pierce me and drain my blood back to the foundations of the tower.

Andrea, you tell it differently, straight out, with a flick of the wrist. But I get sidetracked. And now that I've begun talking about Laff... He's irritable these days. Restless. The uncertainty while he waits to hear on job applications. Resentful. Fed up with me. With "the situation." In a way we all are.

It would have been easier if Bob had raged, knocked over the furniture, smashed the dishes, run out and gotten drunk. But he just retreated a bit farther into himself, silently. A few more inches toward closing the door.

The air has cooled, fog pours in from the shore, from India Point, where the land grows sandbanks out into the water, crowds it off. The water moves and brings back memory. Water. And again water. And the gulls cackling—but then they swoop out over the waves as if to conciliate. I run my finger along Bob's back. As long as I can touch his skin what do I need to say.

Meanwhile Laff lunges at the piano like an overripe cloud and works up a hurricane of the wildest, harshest dissonances. With an occasional, tantalizing haze of a melodic line hovering on the edge of a precipice. He wallows in torturing my ears. Violence, pleasure and vertigo. Until finally he bangs both arms—fist to elbow—on the keyboard as long as he can stand it.

THAT PREGNANT WINTER

Josef and Frederika visited his brother. Uncle Georg, or Schorsch as he was called. Aunt Margaret took an instant dislike to Frederika's bobbed hair and short dress. Margaret still wore long black voluminous skirts over her large hips, even in the middle of summer. A tight bodice with long sleeves, rolled up to the elbows during the worst heat. And a kerchief, starting right over her eyebrows, tied back in the neck. Even so, our parents were given the master bedroom with the fireplace which now housed the huge cradle that had rocked Schorsch and Josef and their father and grandfather. Generations of Seiferts, of millers and farmers.

Frederika stroked the heavy carved wood.

"I'll put our baby in the family cradle," said Josef and lifted Frederika into it for a little joke.

At this moment the lights went out.

"Suddenly," father told me later, "it was as if everything were relentlessly moving away from me. I was left in a gap, a void. Alone. Afraid. I don't know how long it was before Frederika said in a small voice I've never heard her use before or since: 'Help me.'

"I found the door and got Schorsch up to check the generator. Once the light came on I made it to the cradle where Frederika lay curled and very pale. She had felt unable to move a finger, caught in some limbo of greyness.

"Then she threw a fit. Nerves. Screamed. She would not stay in the house. And the next village 10 miles off. Schorsch had to get the horse out and drive us through snow hardened into reefs. The air sharp enough to cut your lungs."

Mother never went back. That was just as well. A farm is not a place she knew how to move in. She would have stepped on any misplaced rake. The wrong way, you know, on the teeth, so that the handle would hit her in the face. A foreign country whose rhythm and language she could not master. Scanned by the sun and spelled by rain guessed from the shape of clouds. And when it came: the puddles, the mud. None of her eighteen pairs of shoes were designed for such conditions. The tortuous paths between odd fields. Winding brooks. Sudden steep rises. Not the clean geometry of room within apartment within building within block within town. A confusion of movement that did not mean freedom to her.

Chance dives into memory. Stray scenes. Details. But in profusion. Thousands and thousands of them. A sea rising, swelling the brooks and rivers far into the land. This is where I would fish for the infinite if I had your or father's craving for it.

ANDREA, WHY DO YOU KEEP HARPING ON BOB?

You don't know Bob in his withdrawn state. Bob with a book. Or without. Like now. Watching the color fall from the trees. It is an easy fall, darkening quickly, with winds light and variable. The intense concentration in his face, nearly a sense of wood, a statue, so contained. Though the phonograph unleashes a storm of strings.

Silete, silete venti, the soprano cuts through.

Bob doesn't have anything against female voices. On the contrary. But mother never tried to sing for him. By that time she had given up. I know this soprano reaches him with her words, *be still, winds*. Takes him into the space of an aria, a poignant andante. *O fortunata anima*.

If I asked: "How can you like Wagner and Handel both?" he might surface as out of a fog, or a cloud of flour like uncle Schorsch. Might mumble something or just look lost, like a modulation in a Puritan hymn, and sink back into his pocket of thought. His fastness.

Oh, he comes out of it. Like a raider, sweeping me up in his arms. He may even listen to my playing for a while, nose around my scores, my books. And then carries the loot back to his stronghold.

Of course I'm exaggerating. Dear Bob. Beloved Bob. But I've resented that he has defenses where I feel like open country, at his mercy. As old Billings said: "the tenor is a flight of fancy, and the other parts are forced to conform to that by partaking of the same air, or as much of it as they can get."

Sometimes I think I would have to leave to get close to him, that if it were possible to be with him while not being there... Maybe this is part of what pushed me toward Laff. If I spread this too-much-of-me around? Won't it become less of an obstacle? No, this is nonsense, and besides there seems, rather, to be more of me. I'm holding on to Bob with the increased force of my own body *and* Laff's. The way mother held on to Josef? I hope not.

I THINK OF FATHER

in those moments. Off in his astral spaces. Preoccupied with the line from mars to moon, jupiter in conjunction with venus in the ascendent, the circle around the fifth house tangential on the mars-moon axis, and the moon's trigonal reflection of the sun. An ordered space in which a stone's falling, the orbiting of planets and a man's death are all the same process. Absorbed. More and more. By a space that is nowhere, not having an object, by a space that does not exist, yet absorbs its observer.

Mother, too, had her castle: of work. Time to peel the potatoes. Time to hem up this dress. Hand me the broom. Who's minding the twins? Vigilant against any break in her routine: the spoons before the forks, the batter stirred clockwise. A fortress of trumpeting action, of hour hand and minute hand, sealed into her muscles, a ringing corset. Curtain crashing down: store hours 9-5. As long as you're only reading you might as well help with the laundry.

Small tasks. Small tactics. To shield her against Josef's cold space. To fence off her air, as much of it as she could get. Things she could do, that Josef didn't dare disapprove of. No "can't you stop this scrubbing?" Even though her wet rag drove him into the corner and out of the house.

It's funny, until last year I hadn't thought much about the past. Roots! I was after branches, leaves, buds. The present and the future. What I would and could do. But now, as the motive is taking shape, as the implications of the tones are less ambiguous, the possible continuations more limited, now, as the pattern emerges, yes, I look back. For instance, to the one scene Josef told me about

HIS MOTHER:

He sat in the barn and played with a box of matches. A pretty box with a landscape painted on it. He remembered sandy ground, heather, pines, a blue lake. Not at all like the craggy hills and rocks around the farm. He did not just look at the box. He tried to make a sunset behind those pines when his mother happened to walk through and "without saying a word hit me across the face with a wet towel. I certainly deserved it. I might have set the barn on fire."

One action only. A whole life, a whole person. Like Frederika's father refusing her singing lessons. Like King Pippin's daughter dropping her handkerchief from a window of castle Schwanberg. Less elegant. Slapping her child with a wet towel. He kept her photo on the wall. Three quarter face in a dark peasant kerchief against a background of ivy. Dark dress buttoned up to the neck. Not old, her face. Nothing to make you say: grandmother. Or: let me help you. Not smiling. Self-contained, silent, her face does not demand attention, but takes on the color of the afternoon around her.

ONE ACTION.

Swatting Josef. Small wonder that he left all the spanking to Frederika. Who performed the ritual inexorably and with energy.

"When the hand on the clock reaches the '2' you will have eaten your spinach or . . ."

Her lips tightened. Her hand gripped mine, dragged me into the living room where I had to kneel at the couch right under the big painting of Richard Wagner at the piano, with all the figures from his operas rising cloudily from the keys. A cane appeared in mother's hand, her small , soft hand. "Nearly indecent, so soft," said my friend Herman later. Too soft for punishment, for the sting across the buttocks.

For years, even after I left home, I would awake from a nightmare of mother coming at me with a lion tamer's whip. Howling with pain as the whip struck my face I marched on her and wrestled her for it. I managed to wake up whenever I succeeded, bathed in sweat, hollowed out. I had to wake up to stop myself from whipping her in turn till she'd crumple in a soft heap.

Then I could not budge. Then I would be in a stupor for hours. Then I could not move my fingers in the small and precise motions needed for a run or trill. Till it gradually thinned out, this, here, a bit, gone, relieved, the difference of a relaxed muscle.

"Rikele, this can't go on."
"You're tired of me?"
"Piffle paffle. But Josef . . ."
"He doesn't know."
"Sooner or later he'll find out."
"Not if you don't blab."
"Piffle paffle."
"You *are* tired of me."
"Rikele, don't you understand?"

He comes less often.
"Men!" Frederika thinks, adding an extra exclamation point: ! "And it might be his child."

"IT'S IMPOSSIBLE

not to be interested in this," said Josef putting his hand on Frederika's belly where a little heel or elbow made it bulge. Outside a splendid spring sun was slipping down behind St. Stephan's. Windows glistened with recent rain, a mild, scented spring rain which coaxed out the first down of young leaves.

"This beginning of life. Beginning and recurrence. An endless cycle. Cell marries cell just as the proteins combined in the nutrient broth. Repetition purifies time into substance. Ontogeny repeats philogeny. The fish stage. The embryo develops gills. He develops lungs also: amphibian fear of shallow water. And in a few months hence," Josef wandered over to the window to allow his vision space and a last ray from the sun, the Eye of Osiris, "in a few months hence, a traumatic cataclysm, a general convulsion, his first sense of catastrophe: his sea contracts and is carried out of its bed. Mountains spring out of the ground and force him down narrow canals. Rivers change their course. He drowns in terror and tubes. All is ruined, the ancient traces effaced. He emerges. He is expelled into another, the aerial ocean. A sea of microbes invades the inside of his body. He screams—"

A clatter of knitting needles. A clacking of heels. Creaking floorboards.

"Time to peel the potatoes."

Poor father. He did not divert his audience nearly as much as himself. Was he in love with his voice as well as with his ideas? It rose to the clearest trill in the astral register. On certain words, like "matter" or "the Ancient Serpent," he could make it grumble like distant thunder and grow to an earthquake that shook the apartment to its corners. It would have dug holes into a crowd. People would have moved off, not as mother did, but as if in fright, showing the square, the macadam with little flecks glittering like mica.

"You haven't come for a long time, Franz."

"Been busy."

"With another woman."

"Piffle paffle."

"You used to come whether you were busy or not."

"Piffle paffle."

"And our opera: OEDIPUS RECHTS or THE PLAGUE IN BERLIN?"

"Yes, our opera." Franz started humming. "This might work in the overture. Do you recognize it? Jazzed-up Bach. End of the St. John

Passion. *Ru-het wohl, ru-het wohl* à la Stravinsky. A little syncopation. Or it might be good to use when our Tiresias comes in. Oracle—chorale, you see?

> Young man, yo-ung man,
> let's no-o-o-ot be fo-or-mal,
> what you-ou did
> i-i-is no-or-mal.

"Should get Josef in on this for the text."

"But you do very well. Like the plague chorus. It's funny:

> This ain't no life,
> ain't nothing but ache-sistence."

"But we need a scenario, the straight parts. With astral bodies, if need be."

"As long as you write me a nice aria."

"You bet, Jocasta: 'Oedipus Schmoedipus, as long as he loves his mother'."

Old joke, isn't it. I was a little surprised, too. Like expecting a red rose tattoo and finding the ordinary wrinkles. Anyway, this is what I could make out. I'll enclose the sheet. See if you can decipher more from that mess of doodles, converging staves, weaves of crossed-out words.

There is one curious thing: you'll notice Josef's handwriting in the upper left corner:

"CORROSIVE MENTALITY."

Crabbed gothic script, all points and angles. Fanfare: time to be on a war footing, time to chart hostility against desire, first skirmish, spite variants ready to take the screen. One phrase. One Nazi slogan. I wonder when he added it. Before? More likely later, after he found out. When the sun had struck the seed in its patient position between stone and more stone. At least that's what I hope the ground was. How long was the seed in sprouting? Or had he said all along: Franz is Jewish, *but* he's alright, he saved my life? Corrosive mentality. I suppose it refers to the beginning: "Laius meets his son at the crossroad and makes a pass at him." Must have rubbed father the wrong way. Scorched the grass right off the page. Parody was not a mode he appreciated.

"You know what bugs me, Rikele."

"Again."

"Still."

"You want me to divorce?"

There was a startled silence. Then Frederika's triumphant:

"Ah, that called your bluff."

"Rikele, do you realize what a divorce would mean?"

"That *we* could get married."

Franz had a whole list of arguments about the difficulties and drawbacks, the scandal of a divorce. The flagging options, the distracting fears, the social risk, the tribal crunch, the family feud. He also had his customary fap and piffle paffle. Instead, he said:

"And in three months' time you'd put horns on me. Maybe with Josef."

Frederika went white with rage. Slapped him in the face. Franz made a formal little bow and got his coat.

As Uwe did when Doria slapped him. Doria.

OUR QUIET SISTER DORIA.

I am envious of her. Being able to do that. I don't think I could. Too afraid of the violence idling inside me. It might explode the powder keg. Too afraid. The way I wake myself up when my dream has gotten to the point where I tear the whip away from mother. Just before I start whipping her in turn.

I'm trying to put myself in Doria's place. Quiet Doria. Busy mother of five, rushed, distracted, stealing time for her lover, and then... If *Laff* said to me: "Hitler's ideas weren't so wrong?" Of course, the parallel doesn't work. Can't trade situations in the hottest game in town. Laff is perfectly capable of saying this. To provoke. To play devil's advocate. To wag another mask. A flurry of ribbons from his magician sleeves knot into puns or pigeons and slip past me before I can draw a sober breath or cry because it is all illusion.

He couldn't say it seriously. But *if* he said it and meant it, would I slap him? More likely leave. Hand him his hat. Or pants. No, I don't think I could slap him.

WHILE I AM ON THE SUBJECT

of aggression: When Doria had her affair with Uwe I don't remember you grinding axes or teeth in the cause of marriage, home cooking and planned entropy. No matter how small the children, you wrote me from the stronghold of your convent, where I pictured you shocked senseless by Doria's "sin" or gearing your soul for steeper gradients of vicarious penance. No matter how small the children, you wrote me, nobody had the right to demand that Doria stay with Karl. That was before the slap bang end of the affair. What detachment and respect on your part. What largeness of spirit clearing the horizon of your cell and letting the off-season outwit the year with a balmy Indian summer. All this in your walled garden, sheltered from the North Wind which pierces to the bone and which even unclouded sun can hardly temper.

Or were you getting scared? Because you, in a way, had pushed Doria toward marriage? In pushing Doria toward motherhood, did you try to settle old scores with your twin? Reduce her to the role of placenta which is all you wished to have been accompanied by at your birth? And one would think she was in agreement, the way she has gone at it with one pregnancy after the other.

I remember when Karl came to the house to get you. Then to get Doria. He threw me up in the air as you do with a kid of ten. I remember him saying hello to mother in the kitchen. Her feet in a bucket of water. The tub had not worked for years and where could you get a plumber. Her legs were giving her trouble. What times we live in! And the rush of it all. Up the stairs and down the stairs. Now she sat, in the evening, and soaked her feet in hot water. With salt. With mud. With chicken dung. This was Fräulein Voss's recommendation. Had heard it from an old peasant woman and, you know, those folk remedies, there's often something to them. Do not think it was easy to get. 1946. Not a time when you could get anything free. Not even chicken shit. Or for money either. I don't know what father traded for it. Maybe he played oracle for it, used his pendulum on the photo of a missing relative.

But back to your concern for Bob. Is it perhaps simply that you are a little in love with Bob whereas you have long been against Karl? And why? It's only now that he has given you a reason: whereas he could gracefully yield you to Christ as a rival, the more recent "developments" make him dig into the trench of his "outraged moral system" and strike new tremors of oratory to mark the limits of hospitality. His house is no longer your inn. No, Doria has never told me how she feels about all this . . . Quiet Doria.

THE SKY

is darkening, coming down on the city with the threat of the Wild Hunt. Wotan prepares another battle of air. With gigantic thunderheads seething and swelling upward from their inky black bases. The spires remember their Christian duty to fight the elemental forces and rise to hold the heavy threat at bay. Baloney. The Hospital Trust Tower rises higher than any spire in town, even that of Roger Williams' church. To protect its owners' capital against natural disasters? You see what these German memories get me into. Wild metaphors and myths.

I miss father's peopling the land with spirits. With Hun graves, with places of sacrifice and murder, where Charlemagne defeated the Saxons, where a Valkyrie left her hoof print. Sure, I've made pilgrimages: Sarah Whitman's house, Anne Hutchinson's. I've followed Paul Revere's ride, tracked the skeleton in armor, the Buccaneer, the last of the Wamponoags. Gone to visit the Charter Oak. Wyllys Hill. Joseph Wadworth. A crevice large enough for a person's hand to go in. With a roll of parchment. Dramatic enough. But not like Wotan's Oak.

WOTAN'S OAK.

Did father take you there? A dark stump which did not accept the light, it seemed. The wind repeated his name. Wotan. Wotan. Always the same. Whispered. Or howled in a storm. The sky seemed empty above the abbey, drained of its blue. As if its depth had vanished with the god. In mourning for the tree cut down by St. Boniface, St. Kilian, St. Kolonat, St. Totnan. Irish monks.

I remember the day. Gloomy. Fog came in flakes and gusts like smoke from a burnt offering. Father was eloquent. His voice cut planes into the silence.

Here they had assembled, the Franks and Hessians, the people of what is now Geismar, Fritzlar, Fulda, and those from farther away, from Würzburg and Ochsenfurt, Volkach, Ebrach, Wertheim and Miltenberg, from Karlstadt and Brückenau, Kitzingen, Schweinfurt, Gemünden and Lohr. Called by the monks with the red beards who stuck crosses into the air like so many banderillos, daring it to bleed. Monks who got churches and fountains named after them for their pains. St. Kilian's in Kitzingen. The people. Out of the woods they came, out of huts, row villages, heap villages, across the river and down the hills. With horses, with spears, with fur coats. It was the spring equinox. Easter according to the monks. Patches of snow, still, on the mud. And the first snowdrops. Men and women. Brass fibulas and braids. Called to the oak. Wotan's oak.

When they had filled the whole space from the river to the hill —the river Fulda, which gave hard little sounds as it hit against the rock —to the hill where the monks stood with their followers; when they had all assembled King Pippin rode up. Pippin the Short. His daughter behind him. She had not yet dropped her hanky from castle Schwanberg. Shepherd Kitz had not yet found it. Kitzingen was not yet built —let alone the fountain on market square named for St. Kilian, for his part in slaying the oak, for getting his come-uppance along with Boniface, in 754, heathen swords through his body and another through his missal.

Pippin's helmet glistened in the spring sun as he raised his spear to the monks. Song rose on the hill, a flight of open vowels. Wavering breath of the new god, the savior, the redeemer, the way, the truth, the life. Kyrie eleison. Christe eleison.

Howls shot up with the song as Boniface raised the axe.

The axe struck. Struck the oak of the Wild One who rides in the sky, whose name the wind rehearses and the storm shouts out loud, who led them into battle with his horde of mounted daughters. Valkyrie eleison.

The rocks blanched like bones. The crowd fell silent. Drew back from the hill toward the river, the Fulda, as if it could take them away from the sacrilege, out into the open, a long way down to the Rhine, to the sea where the wind galloped unbroken and Wotan still breathed.

The singing went on. Heavy with the thud of the axes. Kyrie eleison. A battalion without weak flank. Forays of crosses into the sky where the white was gaining over the blue, where the white turned ashen.

Only once the singing stopped when toward the end Boniface let his thin voice sail out in a final prayer: "Let God arise, let His enemies be scattered: let them also that hate Him flee before Him. As smoke is driven away, so drive them away: as wax melteth before the fire, so let the wicked perish at the presence of God." The oak groaned and fell. With a wail worse than any storm. Coming down on their heads like a rain of stones. The song rose victoriously, credo in unum deum. *The monks, merciless in their triumph, pushed the crowd into the river, one by one into the Fulda. To be reborn. Into an air cleansed of Wotan's breath. Who will not come back. Whose name the wind will forget. They scattered over the fields, baptized heads bowed to the ground, pursued to the last by the* credo in unum.

It was clear, in the narrative, where father's sympathies lay. You probably didn't let him get worked up like this if he took you there. You were on the side of Kilian and Boniface. Burning for the one God, who seemed such an impoverishment to father. You wore out your voice and exhausted your body in the attempt to praise Him enough. You were fanatical. You would have taken a turn at the axe with partisan cruelty, with a cold and innocent violence, a convulsive passion that knows only its own movement.

This all came back to me, Andrea, a propos a recital in Hartford. One of my best. Started out with Bach and ended with Stockhausen's *Klavierstück XI*. Via Mozart and Bartok. No Romantics, still. Bob was with me, a rare occasion, and read in the town history how Mr. Samuel Wyllys was busy clearing the forest around his homestead in Hartford. He had marked the charter's future hide-out for destruction along with the rest. "But the savages who dwelt in the neighborhood so earnestly begged that the oak might be spared"—and knowing with whom they were dealing, added: "because its first putting forth its leaves had been a sign to them from time immemorial when to plant their corn." Practical, the tides of the trees.

ANYWAY, I'M SITTING HERE

and it's only because I have no definite purpose that I notice not only the encounter preparing in the sky, but the particles of tar and soot and exhaust with which the city prepares the battle, acknowledging herself daughter of the air in her very revolt.

When I say, "no definite purpose," I don't mean I'm giving up writing to you. But writing is not definite like catching a bus, making a marinade, or practicing scales. Not even like trying to conquer

50

Schumann. The course of these sentences doesn't seem to be forward, developing a story, but down. They probe into holes and crevices, dig for roots, sound the walls. You have probably noticed that the only times this begins to sound like a story is when I repeat something father told me, when somebody's lens has already narrowed down the infinite number of possibles, has run the tones together into linear surfaces and projections. Whereas when I find a bit of the past and hold on to it another part slips away.

Like this storm which doesn't seem to break after all. Wotan contains his fury, but goes on unnerving his opponent. The clouds go on gathering. With shadows of all intensities, from delicate grey to deep black, marking the innermost recesses. The whole suffused with a coppery glow while thunder rumbles farther and farther in the distance.

"Franz, I need your help."

"?"

"Frederika's been in some state. Couldn't you come and sing a bit with her? That always cheered her up."

"Piffle paffle. Besides... I don't think I'd be welcome."

"What happened? What did you do? Criticize her voice?"

"Something like that."

"Oh come on. Make the first step. I know she'll be glad to see you."

"Really I don't..."

"Oh please, be a sport. I'm worried, you know, in her condition..."

FRANZ WAS APPREHENSIVE.

He would have preferred to call it quits. A clean slap. A clean break. He was not quite sure of the dam he had built around his head (and heart, he assured himself) which by now said: Ilse Bernstein.

He went only about fifteen minutes before Josef would be home. Nervous and selfconscious, he rang the doorbell.

It was sultry. Heavy with a smell of lilac and coming rain. As he passed the blossoming andromeda by the door he flooded with a sudden premonition of defeat. He saw her before him, "damn attractive," as on the first day when she had thrown down her blouse like a challenge and made his voice jump a fifth.

Frederika stifled a little gasp of surprise. Her belly protruded. Huge. In a dress with white flowers on a light brown ground—the color which became popular six years later: "Hitler brown." A second of silence. It spread through the house. A small pain began to creep up his legs. The clock of St. Stephan struck five.

Frederika's moment of surprise had passed. She pulled Franz to the couch.

"I've missed you," she said a bit throatily, silencing his "piffle paffle" with the melting look she could put into her eyes when she wanted to. It was not for nothing that she had watched *Love* five times in the past few weeks and studied how Anna Karenina looks at Vronsky as she gets off the train. She put her arm around Franz. This was not a moment to square accounts.

"But I knew you'd come eventually. I knew you'd realize what I mean to you."

She arched her back slightly, and her steel blue eyes fastened on Franz's in a way that seemed to plunge straight down to his genitals. Like a bullet. It blew his resolution to be distant into little fragments, flung them in all directions. It left a small round hole in the dam he had so carefully erected.

He tried to think of Ilse Bernstein. So young. So pure and innocent. Maybe even frigid? As if always twirling a white parasol against a clear blue sky. Of course, the parasol was just an image. Ilse, a modern girl, would not be caught dead with such an instrument. She would have been more likely to join in the current fad of nude sunbathing although, as far as he knew, she had not. But Ilse seemed pale as the space between him and Frederika crackled and drew them together. Red fog seemed to rise. His body softened. His perceptions slowed down ...

He made an enormous effort:

"I've come to tell you ... "

She put her hand over his mouth. Quickly. As if the hand knew by itself that he must not be allowed to say whatever he was going to. That small, soft hand. Nearly indecent, so soft. He pushed it off. But its softness, its warmth stayed. A pink blur on his mind.

"I love you," she said.

Her belly made it all the more touching.

I'm sure it was true, too. As she always loved us children truly in the moments we crawled repentantly to ask her forgiveness. Franz was not exactly repentant. But he had come back. The curve leading back to her struck her as form, as beautiful in itself. As a melody tries to leave its origin, modulates to stray keys, but is infallibly pulled back to the tonic. Infallibly, because she did not consider any music later than Brahms.

Franz again made an effort. Like struggling up from half-sleep or from a potent drug which turns your limbs to lead.

"Rikele, I've not come to start over, only to . . . "

She grabbed his arm so it hurt and, her eyes flashing, she said, illogically perhaps, but with a voice which contradicted her haughty eyes and seemed to come straight from her vagina, a voice sexier than her legs with the sun caught on them, sexier than her hips at their most coquettish *déhanchement:*

"If you think you can treat me this way I'll never make love to you again, even if you beg me."

Franz, who so wanted to say: "Fap. Fine with me," suddenly imagined himself on his knees before her, begging, before her crossed legs coming out from under a chiffon dressing gown. He fought the vision, tried to concentrate on the real belly in front of him which stuck out in its proud fullness. But it did not take away, no, it rather added to her attraction, gave it a new softness. And his imagination persisted with her top leg bouncing up and down, her pink toenails dancing right in front of his face.

He suddenly longed for winter, for snow, for a cold white. I ought to be angry, he thought as he felt a wave of hot sweat down his spine, breaking at the coccyx. Putting on airs like this!

Here she moved away, slightly. He heard steps on the stairs. Hopelessly ruined. Josef's arrival was supposed to help him get out. But now, with nothing resolved in any way, with him reduced to a soft, sweaty mass, the husband came in along with an extra strong wave of lilac.

"Hello, Franz. Glad to see you. Have you been making music?"

"No. We've only made up."

The way Frederika said this twisted the knife. Franz felt like a monkey on a leash. Like a little boy caught masturbating. He was frightened by the sheer sexual attraction she had for him. Her power. It seeemed that she held him there, in her body. Captive. In a furry dark. Bewitched. And taking pleasure in it. He knew he would fly back to her tomorrow though part of him wished Frederika were shut up in a cage like the wild beast she was, to save him from coming too close. Now she lay there lazily like a crocodile in her sensual morass, masquerading as a pregnant woman, basking in her power over him. But everything else, even his Ilse, suddenly lacked something. Without Frederika a greyness settled on the surfaces like a fine layer of dust.

"I just read that if the retina recorded infrared rays then on a hot day like this everything would be obscured by a reddish fuzz."

"I feel just like a reddish fuzz myself," said Franz wiping his forehead. "I must be wearing my tropical belt."

"After violent exercise the body would seem to increase in size on account of the heat released by the skin."

Franz wondered if his erection was showing, if Josef was slyly alluding to it. But no. Josef went on innocently:

"The shape of water, rocks, trees would all vary with the season . . ."

Franz knew in a flash where Josef was headed: from infrared rays to ultraviolet rays to cosmic, to astral, to mental, to—who knows—soul rays. Circles within circles, curves and helices, rotational transfer, upward always, the Eye of Osiris and time becoming substance. The fabric of the universe unraveled to show underneath other, quite new crossings of warp and woof. He usually had a certain interest in Josef's speculations. Partly because they were such perfect targets for a piffle paffle. But today he would have liked to pick a quarrel with Josef. He looked at Frederika. Ilse's image receded still farther. He wanted Frederika. Maybe he even wanted the murkiness, the secrecy, the cheating, the double play. He would be back tomorrow. It would start all over. Frederika would again be alternately impulsive and cold, elbows swinging out into the blue air and arms held stiffly to her ice-covered plateau. He did not know which state fascinated him more. Perhaps the coldness which made her seem so complete in herself. Or maybe the moments when this Brünhild melted, when the ring of fire narrowed and ignited her, exploded her into sudden, reckless frenzy. Perhaps the baby would change this.

"THE BABY"

came in the plural. You. Two of you. Twins.

You're right, Andrea. But it is precisely because I do not know Franz Huber at all that I feel free to imagine what went on inside him, to pretend to "render" him with a few traits, a couple of actions. Not a single one, mind you, not like Josef's mother slapping him or Pippin's daughter dropping her hanky. If I make up Franz I may as well pretend to know his mind. With father I'm much more uncertain. Too many years of living by his side. Too many words, too many gestures, too much surface. Below it, below the threshold, he thought, a larger life flows through us. There we vibrate to a larger force. And did he put up with so much because he thought he would finally get in touch with it? All those years in the cold, right by Frederika's side. Did he realize his life closing in? All around him tenement houses smelling of laundry and sauerkraut? With walls painted in the drabbest greys? His fingers hungering to touch her skin?

THEN: AUGUST 2, 1927.
YOU, THE TWINS.

Punctually, a little more than a year after the wedding. Josef was not allowed to be present at the birth, though he felt flesh in upheaval, muscles contracting the whole time. As you sometimes don't see the river, but see, between trees, the light as it stands over the river. With a different quality: water light. He took his shoes off and walked across the dry meadow to the Festspielhaus. No birth in Wagner except with a curse. Siegfried. Blood of the Walsungs. A smell of hay came at him. It already smelled brown, not like freshly cut. And not a trace of moisture in the air.

But twins. A double scar. This is where the trouble starts, thought Josef. This he had not counted on. This double was not ethereal. Too much matter. There was to be time before you, Andrea, before a second child. If there was to be a second. Frederika had overdone it. Always to extremes. She could have controlled herself. He could not control his worry. Tried to run up estimates on raising two girls. His figures remained vague, his calculations acrobatic, as if balancing on a rope. But with one certainty: two would cost twice as much as one. It was like praying for wind and getting a Sirocco, hot, depressing and yielding torrential downpours.

His other calculations were a flying leap beyond even the narrow support of a rope. He had mapped the union of the complementaries: of man and woman, of sky and earth. To bring forth the third term of the Great Triad: child, mankind. A triangle. But now, rather, the mating of consternation and tableau. And the curtain—there was no way of bringing it down.

Further, there were in his notebook diagrams of diamonds whose top, the original ONE, love, divides into the detour of male-female dualism as the longest but most beautiful way to deliverance: the child.

Twins! Two more bodies. Two more weights. Two more branches on the tree of matter. Two more barriers against spirit and sidereal glow. Twins. A shuttle between like and echo, double and identity. His pen edged away from its shadow, its own twin dogging its movement toward broader agreements, spheric prospects.

Pages and pages of crossed-out diagrams. The triangles metamorphosed into molars, fringed curtains, double-peaked mountains. If at least one child had been a boy. A crossing and re-crossing of the male and female would have twined the possession of twins into eureka: here comes symmetry. But two girls.

THREE

is the number of perfection. The odd number pleases the Gods, says Virgil, without even juggling Father, Son, and Holy Ghost. The sacred number, the number which cups the dimensions, the number of power, the cube to which nothing can be added. Or can there? Josef's later speculations on the number four got him onto those other things in heaven and earth that so far were not dreamt of in his philosophy. At this stage of development he wrote:

"The whole measure of time is 3: past, present, future.

"All existence is contained in 3: line, surface, body.

"Man is composed of 3 inner walls.

"We have 3 souls: vegetative, sensitive, intellectual. As well as 3 bodies: physical, astral, mind-body.

"God governs the world with number, weight, measure.

"The triad encloses the 9 orbs, the 9 muses, the 9 months of gestation, the 27 properties of music.

"Jonah spent 3 days in the whale and Christ as many in his grave."

You notice, Andrea, there is no 3-toed sloth, 3 musketeers, 3 men in a boat, 3 blind mice, 3 little pigs. He was a serious man. What do you suppose are the 27 properties of music?

MOTHER?

Filled with a new bravado. The double birth convinced her that motherhood was her special talent. She was the wave of the future. The rising birth rate. The right of young, expanding nations. Reckless apex of hope. I suppose she was even happy. Feeling herself in her swelling breasts. Fondling them as she gave them to you, singing all the while. Milk, the white refuge. Pleasure on both sides of the nipple.

Of us three, only Doria slid into the prepared groove. Quiet Doria. Continues the line of women into the next generation. Hands down the program, the code. Bottle for baby. Cooking three meals a day. Spreading them on clean table cloths. Mother acknowledges her as her only daughter. For what other destiny can a woman dream of but reproduction, the satyr play with a chorus of children. Doria too tired, too quiet to disagree, maybe agrees anyway as she drives her breast into the grabbing mouths. The baby as a source of confusion: forays into contemplation while knitting pink outfits. Better have another to keep herself from thinking. To prepare a future, to mark out the territory, the single small creature, increased population. Five by now. Doria too goes to extremes. Has to outdo mother. Muscles are flexed to the splashing of milk, to the click of the camera for grandma's photo-archive. Costly. The spring palaces gone, the honey ration. Then sleep and quiet, and the price of coffee goes up. Within, shifts in constant formation, natural flavors and cancellation of theory. Doria listened. The two of us made noise. Quiet Doria. Noise is a good thing.

FRANZ WAS BACK

along with the fall rain. Not as much as mother would have liked. If she were not so occupied with the babies she would still feel neglected or have a tighter grip on the conditions. Now she sees him, now she doesn't. Mondays passed without him. The nights turned clear with a white moon. When she tried the ice treatment, tried spreading her polar silence, he shrugged:

"Termite's nightmare: I dreamt I dwelt in marble halls... see you next time."

Went out whistling.

Pretty cool, Franz Huber. The knack of departure. On a small scale. Quick on the pun, the piffle paffle. Suspected of sarcasm. Many of his opinions seemed unsound to his colleagues, un-German. If he had not been such a good musician... Walked off while Frederika, fretful, felt walls moving closer.

Franz Huber. Not as easily hurt as Josef. He did not offer his throat. He had other spaces to move in, more substantial than Josef's astral recesses. Secret beaches where rocky cliffs softened into sand with pieces of amber washed up on it. Bernstein. Ilse Bernstein. Translucent. Air which does not hide the sky.

But clouds had to be reckoned with and are interesting in themselves, of infinite variety and often beautiful. He always came back. A steambath is good for you, especially when followed by a plunge into the ice-cold sea. The Nordic way of health. Franz moved between Frederika and Ilse. Ilse Bernstein. A name. Another name. With a climate more predictable than Frederika's, I suppose. No blizzard driving clouds of whirling snow down on hot desert sand.

I KNOW, ANDREA,

that Uwe meant much to Doria, that he touched the nerve smoldering under Karl's duty-first and no-nonsense. Not that I want to blame Karl. How about the lack of money, the eternal diapers? I know that Uwe meant a cool breeze murmuring, all of a sudden, through the branches, arms swinging in the mild air while the full depth of spring opened out from the throat. You've got me wrong if you think I begrudge her this. I'm only sorry she didn't pick a man with a more acceptable form of misanthropy. So that it could have lasted a bit longer. But then, a married woman falling in love doesn't look for the qualities of a decent citizen.

You've got it the wrong way round. I don't mind that you didn't mind Doria's lover. I mind that you won't grant me the same off-season sunshaft. That you don't admit that I could love Bob, delight in living with him, and yet need another person, a different smell of socks. But don't worry: guilt pours in. That twinge of despair which pulls love toward fear, ecstasy toward sweat and nausea, and which deepens into movement as two voices open their inner parts.

Laff has a job. With the Cleveland Orchestra. Taking his distance. As Franz tried to.

Frederika changed diapers and turned you over. By the clock. Stroked your back, the wisps of black hair. Poked your belly maybe. To see you squirm. It's when the sky dispersed and fog rose from over there where the woods started white with birches and silver moss, it's when you were asleep that motherhood palled and the old restlessness came over her. Then there was nothing to hold her together, no clock or glove, no straight-backed chairs. Gaps in the puzzle. Lacking audience. She was tempted to wake you, to have you cry in order to be able to comfort you and feel herself in your sobs, in the spaces between them as they slowed down.

CHILDREN ARE A BLESSING.

"How are your lovely twins, your beautiful babies?"

Later, two toddlers tied together, in the park where July makes the green monotonous. Small harnesses with a yardlong leash between you. Mother proud of her ingenuity:

"By the time I wiped the nose of one, the other would fall into the lake or stick her finger into a turd."

No, not likely that she would say that.

". . . stick her finger into the dirt."

The possibility of a three step movement away from your twin. No more. Anchored. To what? A mirror image that can take off on its own? An independent shadow? A shape which should be you, but is not? A double trying to get away? A refrain? An echo? Not quite Siamese. You don't have to lie down when Doria is tired. You don't have to pee at the same time. But you mostly do. You stand on four feet in your identical little dresses, wrapped in public attention.

"Look, twins."

"Can you tell them apart?"

AND A LITTLE LATER YET,

four feet running in and out of the house, no matter what weather, what town, what state of the nation. Kids running in and out. You must not step on your shadow. You must not kick your twin. The town is already Kitzingen. With its leaning tower and the fountain where St. Kilian raises both his finger and his sword. Our parents were glad enough to leave Bayreuth, as you'll see presently. But father misses Mime's smithy, the year revolving around the festival, turning over at breakneck speed in the summer, then slowing, the spaces between days lengthening to weeks, to months.

Moltkestrasse. Number 5. Kitzingen am Main. You hated the house.

"I can't stand it," you said, "that dirty brown."

I hadn't thought about the color. It became disgusting once you had pointed it out. "Hitler brown," dirty, greyish where the plaster had crumbled. Big splotches, islands in a sea of slop. You felt each of those like a sore on your skin.

When I went in, the muslin curtain on Frau Enck's door moved with her keen stare. I pretended not to notice, never once looked in her direction. I was terrified, certain that she was a witch, that she could change me into a doorstep or voiceless smoke.

One must be polite with witches: *"Guten Morgen, Frau Enck."* Besides, she owned the building. Got it cheap in 1938: a Jewish house. One of the many wine merchants. The cellar is large, vaulted, its dark still has a trace of Iphöfer Kronsberg and Nordheimer Vögelein. Whereas the smell Frau Enck wore about her was of cabbage, the alibi of being ordinary. Recovering, I tried to get around her up the stairs.

OUR HOUSE HERE IN PROVIDENCE

is nearly a century old. Has gathered in the air and breath of how many people. No wonder that the wind sets the wood creaking, that the walls crack where they've been forced to meet. And when I roll a marble along the floor for the cat its path maps the most unpredictable slopes and valleys.

The other day, though, I thought I heard a louder creak than usual. Somebody on the porch? No bell or knock. I went on reading, but again thought I heard something. I went to the door. Stood there for several moments, uneasy, a little bit afraid, but finally opened. Bob was standing there. Looking at the door as if he had never seen it before, at me as if he wondered who I was, where I came from.

I had seen him stare into the bathroom mirror like this. Not like Narcissus, not pleased: lost. No, not lost either, but searching, breathing some strange light. Gauging the risk of penetrating his own eyes all the way back beyond the layers of quotes from Dickinson and Thoreau and Hawthorne to find perhaps nothing at the center.

I'M RUNNING AHEAD AGAIN, ANDREA.

Between three periods and two languages. Between beds and houses. Analogies and suppositions. One egg like another twin, one memory much like some other conjecture. No system. No proof. No progress. And all to avoid answering your questions about Gillian.

GILLIAN.

What is she like? Younger, of course. Very shy. At that first party I noticed her because she looked orphaned in the middle of all the people and furniture. Held herself so erect she nearly quivered. A beige dress with a broad belt which emphasized how thin and delicate she was, how boyish her hips. She moves with a mixture of caution and a slightly exaggerated looseness, half on tiptoe and half as if the threads were unravelling. A hazy sonority like whole tone progressions, her presence lies lightly on the room. Alarmed when you look at her too directly, her eyes seem to run for shelter and come out toward you only hesitantly, as from a place farther back in her head.

I lured her out. But it was Bob filled up the space. I first noticed his restlessness when he hadn't seen her for a few days. His glow when she was with us. A tenseness, nearly an extra presence. Looking at Bob I encountered a cautious, guarded casualness. Deflected from Gillian on his other side.

One evening after dinner, Laff and I were playing. Laff's cascades pealed off into silence like a film overflowing the reel, loops of celluloid piling up on the floor. He swayed with the sound, shifting his bulk from one foot to the other. Suddenly, as if somebody had turned my head, I looked over to the sofa. The light caught on Gillian's wristwatch, the white rim of a cuff. Bob and Gillian. Holding hands.

Husband. Lover. Friend. I was waiting for those words to come back, preparing my tongue to say Bob, Laff, Gillian, and everything would be as usual. But they didn't come back.

I went upstairs pretending a headache. I knew I had no right to be upset. But pain tears into your body without asking permission.

Now you scoff: has her lover living in the house and howls when her husband holds hands. You're right.

Later, Bob said: "She's like me."

O hell, let's get back to the parents. That's what we agreed on, after all. But am I telling you anything new, worth mentioning?

DO YOU KNOW HOW YOU GOT YOUR NAME?

Names fascinated Josef. Names. Their echoes from the past. *Fredericus rex, our king and lord.* Why did Frederika insist on calling him "Beppo" when he did not like it. When it placed him in the wrong context. Was she trying to mislay and lose him in a landscape too sunny for him to get his bearings?

Your names. Josef went through history and rejected Heloise outright. Agrippina? Imagine grandson Nero. Josephine was too frivolous, Elizabeth too protestant. Helen pretentious, to say nothing of Dido, Semiramis, Nefertiti or Hatchepsut. Fausta: circled. Marie Curie was cancelled out by Dubarry and Stuart, Jenny Lind offset by "spinning jenny." Eleanor marked with an arrow, likewise Beatrice. No appearance of Xanthippe.

Given his love of Wagner and the fashion—uncle Schorsch had already named his children Gunter and Brünhild—I was surprised there was no Siegrun, Sieglind, Siegheil, no Winifred or Wahnfried.

Names are rhythm, says John Barton Wolgamot in his book, *In Sarah, Mencken, Christ and Beethoven There Were Men and Women.* I wish I could find out if he is possibly a relative, a brother or nephew of mother's. Anyway: a whole book made up of names. And printed. Unlike Josef's. A symphony of names. Four movements. A rhythm. A celebration.

The Church, in her wisdom, has coordinated this rhythm of names with that of the stars: a calendar of names. Saints. They were there, in Josef's notebook. With their attributes: St. Barbara with her tower. St. Lucy and her flower. Two eyes on a stem, luminous, living. Father liked her: giving up her eyes for a brighter, unearthly light. But she had to wait till I came along nine years later. St. Agatha, her breasts on a platter. St. Catherine with the wheel that shattered.

But your name was not there. Surprise: it was mother. We have a clipping from the *Bayreuther Allgemeine Zeitung* marked with her peculiar "x" which looks rather like a bow-tie: ∞. The "Andrea Doria" launched on August 2, 1927. There you are. There *you* are. Doria had to be disguised as Dorothea to be allowed into the parish register. The connection no more accidental than that Leo should be in the ascendent. Launched from the stocks, launched through the floodgates into the open time unchecked except for its swelling with the moon. Launched toward the elusive horizon where a setting sun suddenly wheels up to center sky and the blaze spreads.

Names. When I played with Esther, Frau Enck's adopted daughter—this is in Kitzingen, during the war—mother declared:

"It's a shame you're called Esther. Not a nice name. It's Jewish. We'll call you Anna."

YOU SURVIVED

your name. Survived its hitting the tanker and going down. All three of us survived our childhood, fed by what has, now that this period is completed, the fragile charm of things out of reach. Sometimes they take on the coloring of dreams just because I cannot locate them in a precise context. Their ground is the vagueness of memory. And we all agree that my memory is bad.

"Bad!" says Bob. "You have no memory at all."

THE CALL OF THE KNIFE-SHARPENER,

though, cuts through. The grating of blades against the round stone turning, rising and setting in its bed of water. We stopped heaven-and-hell or hide-and-seek in order to watch. Or that other crank which turned out the desperately sad Ännchen von Tharau and the waltzes too heart-rending to tempt even a child into dancing. But the grindstone gathered us in a silent, unmoving ring, huddling against the centrifugal force of time made visible, huddling against visions of severed limbs, of dead bodies in numbers that denied the unique, irreplaceable nature of each, of bones snapped, signals taken back, the machine stopped.

Mother. Sat bolt upright in bed. A kitchen knife in her fist. We must have been there, at the door, for a long time, pleading, coaxing. We must have forced the door, father and I. How? I don't remember. Just a sense of falling. I looked up to see if they were falling also, father and mother. The rope between them couldn't hold. Not both. But they looked straight at each other. Riveted. Not even turning aside once, for me, or as you would do for an audience. If I had been a real audience there would have been a tilt of the head, of the eyes, a smile down and then up at the gallery, a relaxing from the waist in the desire to seem cool, to be charming Frau Seifert who knows how to cut a figure without the help of a knife.

YOU SURVIVED

your birth. Both of you. Even though you were twins. I read that among many tribes, the Ibus, for example, the birth of twins is considered a disaster: the double is a matter of pre-birth or death. You cannot live with it. So if a child does not at birth win the duel with its womb-double, the placenta, if a second child comes out and does not die within a few weeks, the second child must be put to death and buried. Without pomp and ceremony.

Did you enact, without realizing it, some such rite when you entered the convent? You. The younger, the second-born. Tried to put yourself to death? Tried to bury yourself in silence? Secretly. Without pomp and ceremony. But you survived.

You had even learned to lift your head when mother dropped the bomb. Your skill is documented on a dozen photos. With subtitles in baby talk. You had learned to crawl, your eyes fixed on a space beyond the walls, on letters printed in rows. You hadn't learned to walk yet though you could pull yourself upright if Josef or Frederika gave you a finger. But you wanted the whole hand before you would set one foot before the other on this rope between them. You were right. What you needed was a net. For as you pleased one of them the other let you down. Mother with a clunk so your bottom hurt. Josef more furtively, not meaning to, really, the same way he farted, a bit shamefaced, shifting his chair so the chair would take the blame. And when you fell you had to scream.

"Andrea has to make a lot of noise because she's ten minutes younger," goes the family joke. And: "She made so much noise that she got the wrong name, got baptized first."

Noise is a good thing to make. A great thing even. It deafens, it blinds, it numbs the pain. I've often wondered about Doria, our quiet sister. How does she manage? Without our tantrums, our growls, our bursting rages. Are we using up her share?

"Donner and Doria," father swore, inappropriately. As a child, though, she stomped her foot:

"When will I be able to do what I want!"

Another family joke. That she should want to. Silent Doria. Silenced down to her sex. She might have been in a nunnery too for all she felt in that region. Sometimes she was so sure she had inside her another set of walls and wallpaper rather than an organ that her pregnancies seemed frivolous exercises and even the real babies insufficient proof and discouraging. I think this is why she keeps having them. Reckless and on the run. Babies slide through her like a gypsy glissando, like days through the year. Upping the credit line. She too goes to extremes.

LATER, YOU GO INTO CONVULSIONS

whenever you are home. Your whole body screams, silently. You foam at the mouth. How else could you break away your ship frozen to the ice, drifting with mother's direct course into the Arctic wind-divide. I remember the first time, Andrea. At Christmas. At dinner. That spoonful of soup which never reached your mouth became an open sea you tried to throw yourself into, right there, in your chair. A body, rigid and torn between the pull of gravity and a flailing of arms wanting to hold on to the bridge. But you hit the water. You turned blue and the spindrift bubbled up from your mouth. The current was so strong it knocked me down as I ran for the doctor.

But you haven't learned to walk by yourselves when mother

DROPS THE BOMB,

drops the rotten egg, tells Josef about Franz.

Why did she do that? We'll come to it. There are letters. With clues. But you are right to ask. Pure air may be cooled far below its dew-point without condensation of the moisture it contains. Some kind of nuclei must be present for drops of water to form. Dust or smoke particles will do. It was not that she was sorry. It was not that she could not stand the secrecy any longer.

Josef would have closed his ears. *This* noise was not a good thing. No "stop this screeching" could silence it. An obscene, infernal noise, louder than the full Wagnerian orchestra and the twenty anvils together.

He closed his eyes instead. It was a mistake. There were the scenes of the past two years in a speeded-up film. Slipped from the shells of their old meanings.

Frederika in the door frame, hands folded on a green belt. Click. Frederika pacing up and down. Frederika undressing, hastily, against a background of red, suddenly, the blanket on the bed with its silk border. Click. Frederika standing by the piano, one hand on Franz's shoulder. Frederika's eye, blue, fixed on something beyond. His hand on her hips traveling up. His fingers pressing at her back. Click. Frederika, face buried in a bouquet. The back of her hand lifts her hair from her nape. Click. Franz and Frederika amid suitcases. Climbing into the train. Franz's hand on her ass. Himself, fool that he was, with the double stroller. The "imperial" twins. Click.

The teachers' lounge. As he entered, that moment of sudden silence where a syllable dangles dizzily in the unexpected void—and then the rush to catch it, to put a different sentence under it, to hold it up:

"Did you say they are cancelling the final meeting?"

A bit too casual to sound solid. Click.

In temperate latitudes the most frequent type of pressure change in the atmosphere is a fairly steady rise or fall which may last for only a few hours or for as long as several days. But there are also jerks, usually upward, sudden changes of as much as one tenth of an inch. They are often associated with violent phenomena, squalls of wind, heavy showers of rain, thunder and lightening.

Frederika on her back. Franz pushes his hand under her back to open the brassiere. He pulls it off. His left still pulling, his right hand cups the right breast, then gives way to the mouth sucking, gently, on the brown nipple. Only now he pulls the skirt off, the pants. She helps with her right hand while her left travels up and down his back, and his right leg moves in between her legs, the knee pushing in. Between. Click.

His little jokes. Franz's. "How much richer the harmony when the *third* is admitted between tonic and dominant." Between. Click.

Frederika bending over the "imperial twins," the "grossdeutsche offspring." Click.

Frederika naked. Leaning against Franz. Click. Against his hairy knees, his hairy torso, hairy face. Click. Little horns push out of his forehead, his tail comes curving round on the side. Click. Lascivious smile from one ear to the other. Click. Frederika kisses this satyr face, this hairy mass of puffy flesh. Click. Greedy purple, the jaw jutting, from the low, jealous angle. Josef had never thought about how ugly Franz was. Click. Frederika's ass, bare, up in the air, it seemed, Franz's hands on it like tobacco leaves. Click. Frederika's fingers, soft, in the satyr's beard. Click. Frederika's fingers, firm, on his prick. Click. Tongue in ear. Click. Tongue against tongue. Click. Prick out of sight. Click. Finger nudging the anus. Click.

There is a groan. It is Josef's. It is long and drawn out and still goes on in his ears long after he has stopped making a sound. It has fused with another groan, a scream, rather, that he has heard for years: "The Jews are our misfortune." And still his retina: click contract click expand click thrust click retreat click faster click slowing click dissolve and now now click click and himself beside himself beside them taking the picture, taking it all in.

Josef felt crushed. Crushed like a frog on the highway. Then again his new knowledge swelled and distended his body. His memory burst in the too low pressure of the air. Throbbing, rioting pain. A polyp fastening to the tissue of his soul with innumerable arms and mounting higher and higher, up to his brain.

He ran out. If at least it were winter rather than this budding which already stank of coitus and seed, pulp, juice. Or, if it had to be summer, if he could be on the farm. Work it off with sweat and aching muscles. Drop into bed dead tired. He wandered aimlessly through the streets, not knowing where he was going. Flesh. Flesh. Too too solid. Flesh and matter. Become, through sin, more gross. At last, he entered a

CHURCH.

This was not his habit. His own church was the woods and fields. But today he needed the soothing of cold smooth tiles and hard benches, the unmoving stone presence of the old margraves of Bayreuth, the steady light filtered through the colored glass garments of Mary and Josef.

Mary! Who had slept with the Franz Huber of the year 1 BC. The red light! Of course, the red light. To signify the divine presence in the host. If he had been asked he would have recited this phrase without thinking twice. Why had it not occurred to him before, it couldn't be more blatant. The eternal light! The divine presence in every damn whore's window. And did not Jesus take the part of the whores whenever he got a chance? and hang out with them? Why did the Church encourage the poor to burrow into each other's bodies till their kids piled up to the ceiling, and they all starved? More souls for Jesus. Didn't missionaries ring the bells at midnight to wake the natives? For prayer, sure. They might as well have called out: Copulate. Copulate. And the prohibitions? To add the spice of sin? Of fifty seeds she brings but one to bear? A sea of pods exploding softly, bursting like an abbess—abscess, he corrected, but yes, they too, we've heard stories, the whole chorus of hideous fertility, the veins bulge, the weeds swell and spread their shameless flesh, stems glisten with saliva . . .

He groaned. Groaned into the murmur of the two old women telling their beads. Groaned while on the high altar the wooden Jesus pulled his hands off the nails and made horns at him. Solemnly, without moving one muscle of the painted pain in his face.

Josef hid his face in his hands for a long time.

A tap on his shoulder:

"I'm locking up now."

He crossed himself with the holywater and a pang of regret. A beautiful symbol, the water. A symbol. Like the comfortable god he used to bargain with as a child. Whom he could buy with faith and works, the god with his ledger of good and evil. Nature. Life. Sublime and cold energy, caring for nothing, blind, without margin for prayer.

When he got home, Frederika was asleep. He watched her in the dim light from the hall. Plump. Rosy. He could see a whole herd of men, pigs, healthy animals, pass through her. And she would remain unsatisfied. This thought gave him pleasure. He meant it as a curse. She moved, but did not wake up. Her mouth opened slightly. He suddenly remembered how, as a child, he had thought babies were born from the anus. Here he was, shat upon, with twins who maybe weren't his. Who were not his. Who had been rejected by the cradle.

He resolved to get out at dawn before even the twins would wake up.

"Hasn't turned out so well for Seifert after all."

"Sure hasn't."

"Charming Frau Seifert!"

"I guess she was bored."

"That doesn't make it any better."
"No. It doesn't."

"So soon after the marriage."
"I could have told you the first time I saw her. Flirted with anything in pants."
"I hear she was a pretty fast one in Berlin."
"Worked pretty fast here."

Andrea, I half suspected you would challenge "soul tissue." What can I do? Offer you justifications? Descriptions?

THE SOUL TISSUE OF JOSEF SEIFERT THE CUCKOLD:

Nearly square. The woof and warp of purpose and resources. There are remains of creases, but their precise restraint is worn down to fidgets of memory, vanity, *trompe-l'oeil*.

Stains: small patches of sentimental mucus absorbed into the texture, but stiffening it. A trace of blood in the lower left. A clean middle, a sun center of brighter white, shades off through seven spheres of greying emanation toward the raggedy edges where the unity of design is defeated by hazard, frustration, the buying of groceries; where cause and transfiguration show as illusion and decor. Threadbare areas give glimpses of anxiety, the murder of little girls, and the true dark night.

At this time, however, his soul is not in a state to be unfolded: damp, wadded into a ball, it most resembles a handkerchief, used recently, though more resilient than Kleenex.

III

DEAR FREDERIKA,

*I should have known. The way you undressed even the first time,
no trace of shame or modesty —you couldn't wait to jump out of your
clothes, couldn't get it fast enough. The lamp full on you looking at me.
"Charming Frau Seifert," yes. The soft fruit falls.*

*I should have known that you'd always give in to it. The riot in the
blood. Bedroom breath. Only, I thought you had cooled. Apparently
just toward me. Brief as a woman's love...*

*I need some time by myself. I've asked to be transferred. Of course
I had to tell the boss why. Not everything. Just that a colleague had
seduced my wife. He understood. His advice is to withdraw as much as
possible from social life to avoid gossip.*

*I think I was right to tell him. Better that he should hear it from me
than through rumors. With all your talk of freedom —as soon as it gets
known it is judged severely.*

Josef was right in this. The boom of the *Gründerjahre* had given
Bayreuth a few imposing villas, but big enterprise, the major railroad
lines, and liberal ideas had all side-stepped this respectable town.
Tristan and Isolde swooned once a year in illicit chromatics, pulled on
and on by the tonic out of reach. But this was for the tourists. Besides,
as Frederika had pointed out, the singers were too fat to be believed.

In real life it was off color. In real life gravitation, even on steep slopes, was to be counteracted. Men were expected to work. Women to cook, rear babies and pray. Frugality was next to cleanliness, a major virtue. Passion among high school teachers? How could it be supported?

"And his friend too."
"He must have known."
"And twins."
"Her cheek, coming to the graduation ball."
"That was a bit stiff."

DEAR FREDERIKA,

thank you for your letter and the cake. Yes, I miss you, and the kids too. The thought of losing you is terrible. The days aren't so bad. But every morning I'm awake at four. There, alone in my bed, I'm helpless against my thoughts, the poison of deep grief. I keep rehearsing your:
"I love him more than you, Beppo"
"I couldn't have been without him"
"I wouldn't miss the time with him for anything"
till I'm out of my mind stuck on these phrases. And you wonder that I need time to forgive you!

I'm a changed man. I didn't know I had so much jealousy and anger in my soul. Sometimes I feel there's nothing else left in it, no sidereal force, no spirit. One moment I'm frantic and could race across the whole earth in my fury, the next moment I drop from sheer weariness.

I'll try to overcome these feelings. Muddied, thick, unwholesome. Damaging to the aura. And I still love you. The power of the magnet holds. I've always loved you, even though you weren't able to muster any feeling for me.

DEAR FREDERIKA,

No. There was only one single time I was able to take my pleasure with you. Remember the night after Franz's birthday when you were drunk from all that champagne and went wading in the fountain? Barefoot? To put flowers on the triton? That night I decided to have you and on my terms. You didn't seem to feel the jagged stones at the bottom

74

of the basin: I thought you might even be too drunk to notice. That night, that one night you responded. I've often wanted to talk about it when you went back to your old ways. Now I have the added bitterness to know that you had just made love to him, were thinking of him the whole time.

And the times you've hissed, yes, hissed at me: "Leave me alone. You're disgusting." Do you think a man gets over that sort of thing? At the moment I wanted to make love to you? I went back to my side of the bed then, but I couldn't sleep. I kept lying there hoping you'd relent, say: come back, I didn't mean it. But no. Never. Not once. You'd drop off to sleep as if nothing had happened.

You know, Andrea, that in the piano, each note is sounded by two or three strings. But did you know that the strings are not tuned to precisely the same frequency and that most listeners prefer the sound impure like this? The discrepancy, it seems, contributes in unexpected ways to the tone of the instrument. With Josef and Frederika, on the other hand, I would have thought the discrepancy was large enough to keep them from getting together at all. But as with a string, their energy dissipated as a result of friction, the rate of loss proportional to the amount of energy contained. Which was considerable.

DEAR FREDERIKA,

Let me get this contract business straight. You said you threatened to tell the Bernsteins about your affair with Franz unless he paid you a "settlement." Did you just say this to him or did you put it in writing? If in writing, I must have a copy. Really, you go at it like a whore. Wanting to get paid for it. Pensioned off like a royal concubine. If he had fallen for it you'd have taken his money and I'd never have known.

Though if he thinks he can saddle me with twins and get off scot free . . .

DEAR FREDERIKA,

Why do you crush me again and again. "We both loved him" indeed. It kept me awake all night. The time I've known him! You don't know how close men get in a war. And flying together. Barely twenty, we were. Side by side in the open double-deckers, burning on the wind. The fury of rising. The ground lost its power, its hardness, as we rushed up into the air. Intense blue, deep, nearly violet. Or padded with moisture. Like tearing through cold steam. Repelling gravity with will and motor. An unnatural effort. Levitation. And facing death together. The sidereal light. For all his piffle paffle I'd have laughed if anyone had told me he'd cheat on me.

But it's true, he never took anything seriously. Why would friendship be the exception. I mean we all patted the plane on the nose and said "good birdie" and silly stuff like that. Or joked about Jonah when we went out in our "whale." But his jokes went deeper. How he made fun of the parading, the goose-stepping, the oh-glory-sword glinting in the sun. He kept putting on his cap the wrong way round, the shield in back: "To keep the lieutenant from breathing down my neck!" You've heard him carry on. You know what he's like. And the time he fell out for reveille in full uniform and ballet slippers! Can you see the whole row of boots —and the pink slippers! He got into real trouble over that one.

Then again, when we were shot down... I've often told you. He could have tried to save himself, we weren't that far from our line. But he made me a brace and stuck with me. Blood brothers. But now that I think about it, perhaps he didn't mind being a prisoner. He liked the French. The Jews are like that. They don't have our feeling about the fatherland. No real roots. Nothing is sacred to them. Why should friendship be. And yet, of all people. My Blood-brother.

This is the trouble with you too. No religion, no values beyond the material. This is the greatest hindrance to spiritual development. Unbelief checks the action of the will. No child could learn to walk if it weren't convinced it was possible. You live for the moment. Oh, you can be good —but your good actions are like the few isolated words of Italian you've learned, not held together by a system of a higher order, a moral grammar as it were. That's why your good actions hold no more pleasure for you than your whims and sensual gratifications. They lack the higher context. I have sometimes wondered if it isn't a moral defect in me to desire you.

How about this, Andrea? Enough to cure anyone of wanting to be "good," isn't it. And the voice under the words! I'd prefer yelling. An axe in the wilderness. Mother probably resented the slight on her

Italian more than anything else. The rest she had heard before. It had already compressed her ice into a transparent glacier. The "higher things." A bit frequent in Josef's discourse. And in this instance they didn't even have the value of spectacle: no astral bodies slipping in and out, no earths in upheaval, stars in collision, big bang and little whimper. Let alone

THE SIDERIC PENDULUM

which makes visible the vibrations that rule the universe, the mutual influence of heavenly bodies and the earth, vibrations too fast and subtle—or too large and slow—to be perceived by our senses unaided. This is more than just folding back the skin for a glimpse of blood pumping through organs. A deeper exchange.

A thread, weighted with a piece of metal. Father's more advanced model (which Bob now treasures): a delicate chain ending in a small metal cylinder with a protruding needle.

The thread is held between two fingers. Not like playing the piano. No strength and weight from arms, shoulders, back. Again, father's more elegant chain has a little ring to slip over his index. The pendulum will also work without contact to a human body if there is another source of energy. It can be connected to a lightbulb, for instance. Or you can build a "Rumkorf apparatus" where the pendulum is suspended between two brass plates which are connected to a battery or inductor:

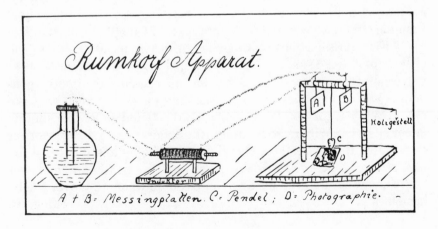

Rumkorf Apparat.

A + B: Messingplatten. C: Pendel; D: Photographie. –

This to convince the sceptic that Josef does not move the pendulum with his hand. For it moves. *Eppur si muove,* Josef Galileo stamps his foot. Threatened. Not by the rack, but ridicule.

"Vibrations? Higher planes? Astral envelopes?" says Dr. Knottinger. "Regression, my dear Seifert. Regression and superstition."

Dr. Knottinger, his own "anguish of the soul" behind thick lenses, tortured by the "imponderabilia of fate and history," but not by astral spaces.

"Watch it, Seifert. Superstition weakens the intellect."

"Superstition? Your sciences! However exact, they must come to nothing for lack of comprehensiveness. In no branch can they demonstrate the origin and ultimate of things. And as soon as the thread of matter breaks, as soon as their one clue is lost, they recoil in fright from the Incomprehensible. Plato, on the other hand, or take even Newton..."

The pendulum moves in circles, clockwise, counter-clockwise, in ellipses, in straight lines connecting my hand and the object, straight lines separating them. The polarity of fields, their secret divisions and attractions. The black snake of matter uncoils into the realm of time. Instant and recurrence. Josef moves, upward always, unaware of his precarious foothold. Only if he encountered an obstacle, only then, by the violence of his fall, could he know his distance from the solid ground. But the obstacles are elsewhere, not in this world of his own devising, where the pendulum kept going like a perpetual melody, and Josef mapped on enormous charts the movements which occurred between my right hand and a rose, a chair, an apple; my left hand and the same; a watch which had been carried by him, by mother, a friend, a stranger, male, female. A sample of earth from the yard, a pebble from the street, sand from the river, a splinter from the bannister.

Lists. Classifications. Taxonomies. A dictionary of relations. The ecology of magnetism. It is now, always, that the pendulum starts to move outward, takes and retakes, inscribes its order of correspondences and symmetries, pressure building up as in a verb or dissonance. While it got dark, and I got bored. I listened for mother shifting in her chair in the living room, the rustle of her turning the page of her magazine. Mother, restless, unstill, but indifferent to the fact that she was, as Josef concluded, wrongly polarized. The pendulum held over her hand always described a figure opposite to what it did over Josef's hand or mine.

BOB NOW TREASURES THE PENDULUM.

Plays with it for hours. And Laff is gone. It's getting cold. With a smell of fall in the air. Already. Laff's absence clings to the house.

Bob had the gall to suggest Gillian move in. In her presence. He stood at the piano, picked at a scale without pushing it towards melody or consequence. He didn't look at me.

Gillian did. And after just a fraction of a hesitation said no. She didn't think she wanted to move.

I was relieved. And a little worried about how much my face told. The evening stretched into pauses. Schumann was on the phonograph: *Ich grolle nicht...*

"What is 'grollen'?" asked Bob.

"A mild form of being angry."

"So she's saying: 'I'm not in a mild form of being angry?'"

Then Gillian started talking about Laff. This is not like Gillian. She is not one of those friends who come running the moment something goes wrong and stick their finger into your sore.

I sometimes suspect you of it, Andrea. Sometimes I think the parents are a pretext. What you want to know about is Bob and Gillian. Even Laff, now that he's gone. The way you wanted to know the exact details of my spankings when we were little. You are hurting and want to see me hurting too. You want us stumbling at one another on a bleak little island, wrecked, both of us, in the intimacy and isolation of pain. Shall we put on head-dresses and pick up the drums? Shall we brandish our knives and have ourselves a little exorcism? Bury our miscarriages together? Our twins, our unwanted selves, our rivals, husbands, lovers? There is more than one witch in the family. We're both her daughters though you still try hard to be Josef's child only.

Shall I admit that my nightmare now is of mother sitting bolt upright in her bed with the kitchen knife in her hand. And the next moment, it is me in her place, wearing her brown velvet dress, my eyes riveted on father and mother breaking down the door, on Bob and Gillian breaking down the door, on Bob and Laff breaking down the door. I'm in a panic to wake before I know whom I am pointing my knife at, in a panic to wake before I strike.

DEAR FREDERIKA,

Franz wants to sue for blackmail. Please: is there anything in writing *that mentions money beside that "contract?" Try to reconstruct exactly what you said in it. What madness not to make a copy. What madness to write it in the first place. Did you take him for enough of an idiot to sign such a thing? Did you or did you not threaten, in writing, to inform the Bernsteins of your affair with him if he did not pay a "settlement?" Did you mention a precise sum? We may have to bring counter-suit. Am very uneasy about this, but must defend my honor. Nice pickle you put your husband in. Please be finally frank and tell me everything. Now I can take it—but no more surprises later on.*

DEAR FREDERIKA,

How can you claim not to have known I loved you. No matter how much you think you have to reproach me with, don't forget there have been a hundred times more kindnesses. You have to take all of me, not just remember the quarrels.

Sound pressure is strictly physical. But loudness is another matter. Depends on how the nerves respond. And the brain. One man's whisper may shatter another's ear drum. But it takes an opponent to learn our own shape.

DEAR FREDERIKA,

Yes, I was always pleased with your gaiety. But also paralyzed. Because you change from one second to the next. It's like sitting on dynamite. I have wondered, the way you have to give in to every impulse, whether you might not simply be morally underdeveloped. Unweeded garden goes to seed, you know. I still remember how you laughed when I explained how this damages your astral body.

DEAR FREDERIKA,

You can take care of my jealousy, my "state disjoint and out of frame," by telling me everything. If there's yet more to say let's say it.

Only then will my imagination be at rest and I'll be able to trust you again. And perhaps we will, through this trial, transcend our sensual love into a higher, more beautiful love yet. A love of understanding and forgiveness. A "gentle and unforced accord." This would be the marriage I'd want.

DEAR FREDERIKA.

Schorsch and Margaret have had another boy. I'm going over for the christening. A Father Doppler is doing it. The new priest in Münnerstein. May work to our advantage. I found out that he is Chaplain Herbig's uncle. About whom I know a few things. I may as well tell you: Herbig is homosexual. I once caught him in the act with a colleague. Rosenthal. Fine kind of catechism. Now the uncle has all sorts of connections which he might be willing to use in exchange for my leaving the nephew alone. What a scandal, though. A priest and a teacher.

TO THE CHRISTENING.

Josef got on his motorcycle. Wrong. He didn't have that until later. By train then, an hour or so. His good suit rolled up in his rucksack. No telling whether they'd be able to spare a horse for him this time of the year. Better be prepared for the ten mile hike on the dirt road. No problem on a day like this. Sunny. No cumulus in the sky. Nice breeze, the kind caused by convection currents from the warming ground. It would give him time to think of how to broach the subject with Father Doppler and just how much of it.

One unnecessary word might ruin it all. It would not even have to be bugger or whore. Might start another story yet. As, in fact, it did. But Josef does not know that. He only worries that it might prove a dead weight. A dead weight is a good deal heavier than any other. How can he be sure it isn't a corpse on his back, this other story which started before his own and is not finished. Because he does not want it to be finished. When the whole space is filled with interlocking stories the problem is to find some margin between them where he can keep himself out and yet show Father Doppler how they connect.

The next morning was Sunday. Harvest or not, both horses were harnessed and the whole family climbed into the cart. White sleeves and embroidered hats and black skirts with red flowers. A bit bumpy, the ride. Not a landau that the Seiferts rode in, an ordinary farm cart. But Schorsch was driving himself, the whip across his knees, lit his cigar as proudly as the mayor himself. He was in his shirtsleeves, but his vest with the gold watch lay next to him on the seat. For church.

Today he did not even think about who owned which pasture or who would sell and how much. He did think a little about who had had his grain ground at the other mill. Also did not seem to see the willows along the brook or the junipers that creep out of the crevices in the rocks. Nor did he bother to take in the beauty of the steep rise of St. Magdalen of Münnerstein way up on the rock. Steep. But he gave the horses a fillip and a cluck of the tongue, and up they went right to the front of the church.

They were already there, waiting. The Hofmanns and Sauerleins and Willingers and god knows who else, customers, neighbors, relatives.

"Beautiful boy."

"Spitting image of Schorsch."

"No, the eyes take after Margaret."

The font is just to the right of the altar. Above it, a wooden Mary Magdalen is put in her grave by three angels and a bishop, in a wooden wilderness. Her body all covered with dense wooden fur, curled tightly over the breasts and bulging belly whose heavy curve is finally allowed to give in to its weight. Dense fur, curled tightly except at the knees and elbows. Even so, and even in death, she holds a hand over her crotch. The wooden bishop does not seem to know how modest she is. Head thrown back, eyes fixed on the sky, he does not dare look where he has his hands under her thigh and buttock. A relief, *gesniten auff zwey oder drey finger hoch*, cut into linden which, over the centuries, has darkened nearly to the color of teak.

A nicer, more solemn baptism than that of the twins, Josef thought. They still knew how to do things, here, in the country. Or was it because little Siegfried accepted chrism and water with equal placidity—not like Andrea who screamed herself purple, screamed herself into first place in baptism.

In the center of the altar, a fully sculptured Mary Magdalen is taken to heaven by a turbulence of angels whose bodies are covered with scales. Magdalen's belly still bulbous, still weighs her down, all gravity and relaxation, holds on to the earth, its vegetable persistence. But her breasts have shed their fur and stand out smooth, round, nipples erect, though on the left one there is a vertical crack in the wood.

82

Josef started writing a letter in his mind.
DEAR FREDERIKA,
I've always loved you(r breasts).
"Amen," confirmed the priest.

Aunt Margaret wept and wiped her nose on her sleeve. Kept it up all the way over to Wiedemann's "Goldener Adler." There she sat between two fathers, her own, old Meinhart, and Doppler. Maier, from Unterhausenstein, sat next to Schorsch. They must have made it up about that path along the brook. Frau Sauerlein leaned so far over the table that Josef wondered why she did not just lie on it as she talked at old Meinhart whom nothing could distract from his bratwurst and beer. Frau Sauerlein was from Swabia—they are all gabby down there. Wiedemann had joined the party *zur Feier des Tages* and let his wife, Marga, take care of the service. Here she came again, Marga, six *mass* of beer in each hand, elbows braced on her hips, laughing, red in the face.

HOW WAS JOSEF

to get at Doppler. And where to start. Right at the beginning? With:

"Franz, there's a rumor we have homosexuals on the staff."

"Piffle paffle."

"Kruger says Rosenthal..."

"Piffle paffle."

Of course, Josef admitted, Kruger is not the most reliable. Half reassured, half taken down as he often was with Franz.

"Still, it's very annoying for the school."

"What is?"

"The rumor."

"What rumor?"

Josef would have explained again.

No. This did not seem essential. Rather start with the time when Franz had forgotten a score and they both went back to the music room. There they were, Chaplain Herbig and Jakob Rosenthal. In the act. Disgusting. Josef remembered mostly the chaplain's head thrown back, all chin and jawbone, his adam's apple bobbing up and down over the white collar. Then the sudden jerk forward, eyes swimming into wide open terror.

Meanwhile Becher, the village teacher, had arrived, late, dragging his wooden leg as Josef would do later, eager for his free drinks.

"How did he behave, my future pupil?"

The question was drowned in:

"The *Mark*'s going down again."

"With 59 more years of reparations to pay."

"We've started bringing in the rye."

"Hindenburg, that old geezer..."

"You going to vote on the war guilt?"

"Stabbed in the back, I say, stabbed in the back."

"We work and work, and it's all eaten up by the interest."

"All goes to the Jew in the end."

"Yes, perforated as we are by a people deeply alien to our national character..."

The teacher, Becher, smirked: "Thought I'd gotten out of the sermon."

"Hallelujah."

That was Willinger. He was happy and drunk on his beer and schnapps.

But Josef had gotten a cue. "A people deeply alien to our national character." Now just wait till Doppler has to step out. Couldn't be long with, how many, four beers, six?

"Excuse me, father, an urgent matter..."

"I'm in the confessional from..."

"It involves your nephew, father, Chaplain Herbig."

Josef was amazed as he entered the study. The parsonage, sure, it was the same old house. But the study now went out onto a glassed-in veranda. The furniture, elegant mahogany, how Frederika would have coveted it. A man of taste, Doppler. And oils on the walls. Not the washed-out reproductions of Caspar David Friedrich, not that pale sunset which old Father Baum had used to prove the existence of god to little Josef.

Father Doppler offered a cigar, Josef his story.

"I am deeply distressed. But I don't quite see what this has to do with..."

He saw it alright. The scene. The priest and the teacher. A corner of a classroom. Rosenthal? Two witnesses. Difficult. Most difficult. But what was this Seifert after?

Josef came out with it, simply.

"If it comes to a trial, I shall have to bring this up. To show Franz Huber's... how shall I say... frivolity in sexual matters, how he corrupted... I don't mean physically, not like what Rosenthal did to your nephew... but morally... I mean, Chaplain Herbig and I, it seems to me, we... we are both victims... Jewish perversion and..."

"But you didn't report it at the time."

"That's just it. I may have failed in my civic duty. But it was Huber persuaded me. Christian charity, he said. Christian, mind you. Ruin a man's life for one fall into temptation. Consenting adults. Between them and god..."

Franz's arguments. They had gone on all night against Josef's:

"But it's a crime."

"But a teacher."

"Our first and foremost duty is to protect the young in our care."

And finally:

"Franz... are you... I mean, you yourself..."

Franz had roared with laughter. He had spilled his wine, choked, guffawed:

"You of all people should ask me!"

And then had suddenly sobered:

"I'm about to be engaged. To Ilse Bernstein. Don't tell Frederika yet. I want it to be a surprise."

Father Doppler was still at sea:

"But what exactly do you think I can..."

There we are. Finally.

"Am I mistaken to assume you know Ministerialrat Wehner?"

"Not at all. We're fraternity brothers."

"Well. Huber is engaged to Fräulein Bernstein. Of Bernstein and Wolf. Yes, exactly. Big money. Which means that, if it comes to a trial, some judge like Hatzfeld will take an interest in the case and be prejudiced in their favor."

"I see. Yes, our laws give insufficient protection against these dangers from within."

"What I hope for is a settlement out of court. Failing that, delays, and assigning the case to a sympathetic judge. Kessler might be the man. So I thought I'd ask..."

"You've done well to come to me. I shall write to the Ministerialrat."

"A REAL GERMAN,"

Josef hummed to himself on the way back to Oberhausenstein, drunk with his cunning as with cheap liquor. The virtue of the curve, the oblique approach. He did not mind that the cart had long gone, that he had to walk the ten miles back to the farm. The cool Sunday evening dropped down from the rocks and softened the points of pines and junipers. The world was beautiful. He did not even mind that the family had already finished supper. He stretched his legs under the kitchen table and ate what was left. Then he sat with Schorsch over another beer. "Fine man, Doppler. A real German." Until Aunt Margaret called sharply:

"Time for bed."

Josef took a step, a bit unsteadily. But he made it to bed. This night he dreamed of Mary Magdalen.

She comes toward him, her head heavy on her neck, her breasts wet with tears.

"O Beppo, Beppo."

Her color is paler than this morning, nearly white. No wormholes.

"O Beppo," she sighs, "Time flies in flocks of angels. But it is always now that my penance begins."

Tears pearl out under her heavy eyelids. She bathes his feet in her tears and dries them with her hair.

"O Magdalen," he says as he caresses her, "your breasts are smooth without fur."

Throngs of fluttering wings on the telegraph wires. He continues:

"It is always now that we become like fish."

Long after, an electric blue.

Was it an accident that Josef, at this time, gave up parting his hair in the middle, his "popo part," and began combing it onto his forehead? Like Napoleon. Or Caesar.

DEAR FREDERIKA,

It was a good idea. Time for all Germans to stand together. I've always loved you. If I could only believe you're sorry.

How hard the sky is today. Steel grey. Harder than mother's eyes. Harder than the houses on Benefit Street, though they are proper, close-mouthed, with prim columns like Puritans checking their ledgers. The wind is from the Northwest: no tang, no salt to it. A smell of carbon monoxide that the grass is too saturated with to drink in any more.

The relaxed feeling of being dirty. Not scrubbed, not up to snuff—do you think Josef felt like this? Wallowing in a wrong agreement with himself. Outsmarting them. It relaxed his gut. The world was alright. You don't know that state, Andrea. You're always up on your toes, or if you get down you're miserable about it. Doria too. Two baths a day. Soaping Karl's touch off her skin? Rinsing the children away? Part of herself? Trying to get down where she might, according to Josef's gospel, be in touch with the larger life?

JOSEF WAS TRANSFERRED TO ASCHAFFENBURG.

Farther West. Against the prevailing winds, but carrying his temperature with him. He was not thinking of the French troops moving in the same direction, beginning to withdraw from the Ruhr and Rhineland. Not chasing them. Chased, rather, by this dog of an affair wagging its tail for all to see. Josef ran harder, seeing murder in its heart. His reputation. His honor. The train moved along the Main river which also moved westward, toward the Rhine, a shimmer of moving reflections, white points, little heads of foam. Its calm lack of anxiety pearled off Josef's like so many drops of water.

DEAR FREDERIKA,

You write me, "Beppo, I can't be without you." And I can't help grinning. Need I remind you: Berlin, May 26. Speyer. The June excursions. All your Mondays.

It wasn't out of concern for me that you stopped. Or remorse. You would never have told me if Franz hadn't broken it off. Or if he had paid you a pension according to your contract. You want to take revenge. Prevent his marriage. You want me to ruin him. You may end up ruining both of us. I'm legally responsible for your "contract."

The more I think about it the more I feel it was much more your fault than Franz's. You must have encouraged, even forced him. May I remind you of your: "Yes, it tempted me." Admit it. It isn't love or remorse that drives you to me. It's jealousy of Fräulein Bernstein.

Yes, you always took good care of my household. But have you ever bothered about my feelings? There's more to marriage than the smell of good housekeeping. Even the nourishment of the body comes not merely through the stomach, but also, imperceptibly, through the magnetic force which resides in all nature and by which every individual member draws its specific nourishment. Here's where you starved me. When I tell people about "my" wife they're appalled.

I don't seek new quarrels. I seek peace. But it's up to you to regain and deserve my love. You are the one who destroyed it. I don't want to divorce. I love you in spite of everything. Why else do you think I'm suffering so. But I will put you on probation. I can't go on as before.

I feel so much better here than I did at home. I get up in good spirits rather than paralyzed from the start. I'm beginning to meet people. The colleagues seem alright, and the women don't seem to think I'm so bad. Especially a little blond Prussian is very nice to me. I might end up falling in love with her out of gratitude. But you don't have to worry. It's not tit for tat. My reason and sense of duty are stronger than my sensuality. You may end up being grateful to this woman yourself. You had made me transparent. I didn't exist. Now I'm again taking on a body.

DEAR FREDERIKA,

I'm sorry I mailed the last letter. Yes, I'm still bitter. This will remain a shadow on our marriage. But I love you and will do my best to make our staying together possible.

I'll hear about the apartment in a day or so.

Cold, gloomy days are only too frequent in the temperate latitudes. East winds and overcast skies may continue day after day, and the sun is obscured and has little effect on the temperature which is hardly higher by day than it is by night. In 1929, there were as many as seventy-eight days on which the sun did not appear at all in Bayreuth or Aschaffenburg. The palls of cloud remained unbroken for weeks at a time.

DEAR FREDERIKA,

I must say I'm outraged by your dragging third persons into our affair. Who are they to judge. Any fault is commensurate with the suffering it causes. I alone am judge of that.

You always listen to others, to anybody rather than me. Like the time when you stopped nursing and wanted a vacation in Berlin. That famous vacation. Your "honeymoon" with Franz. Fool that I was to send Franz along so you wouldn't be bored. That's what you were so afraid of: being bored. Because it was the country which anybody reasonable would choose for a rest. What a fool! Sacrificing myself, taking care of the babies. You might as well have gone to Berlin. But you had to write to Frau Prell, whether I was justified in refusing Berlin. And when she took my side, of course, you wouldn't show me the letter.

Yesterday I sat over a beer, very gloomy. A woman from the next table came over and talked to me, stroked my hand. Why couldn't you ever do something like this? Like the Saturday after the rehearsal when I came home depressed. You couldn't even ask me what was wrong. You simply refused to stay home with "a mug like that." Or at night, when I sighed, why couldn't you ever give me just one good word or stroke my head? Instead of taking your blanket to the couch where I wouldn't disturb your precious sleep. Not to mention your constant threats: I'll divorce. I'll move out.

Even just copying the letters for you, they do not seem right. Changed by my thinking about them, by my sending them now rather than right after father's death. As my memory lumbers toward them, the parents retreat a little farther each time. They leave an image I pounce on, happy for a moment till I realize it's a decoy. A decoy I have manufactured. The world vacant because I refused to see it earlier. Powdery snow over lacking ground. By now when I ask just who, what, where, at which moment, I am peering at a blank, a stretch of snow where only the wind combs up an occasional ridge and as quickly wipes it off again.

YET

the parents were there. They lived. They did things, every day. They started out anew. Started out with what is now known. And went on. Length, transition, modulation. Without illusions. Clear air is a poor blanket. The themes unalterable as the composition grows. His honor. It would take Schubert's inventiveness to turn this condition to advantage. He felt his way across the new terrain which remained unfamiliar because he did not mean to get used to it, to let it be unnoticed like the color of walls or an inner hum.

He had her angrily. Never forgot that he'd been had. He fucked her in a rage, wedging his prick into her as if to cork up her womb, to keep other babies from coming out. And getting afraid of succeeding. And succeeding. For a long time. Nine years. His own voyeur, watching now consciously the role he had starred in all along. Watching which way mother goes when she leaves the house. With her short, resolute, nearly military steps. Her white shoes, recognizable in the dark, showed the little turn she made to look back. To see if she was watched? Indication of guilt? Did she think she had heard the kids cry? Too late to give up the trip. One way ticket. Tears and *déjà vu*. Not as many tears in Frederika as he had hoped. "The fruitful river in the eye." Probation. Slow forgiveness "wrung from me by laborsome petition." Not by Frederika. He tapped his finger against the barometer. Two, three times. It showed what it showed.

The decay of their marriage was like that of the sound from a piano string. More complicated than a straight line. The first segment always starts at a high level and decays quickly. The prompt sound. The immediate disaster. Followed by a final slow decay, the aftersound, which dragged on for decades.

Father Doppler had written letters. Three of them. Paced up and down his study for quite a while. Four steps to the window, four steps back to the desk to pick up the little knife and snip off the cigar tip. Three steps to the bookcase, eight steps back to the window. He did not have a barometer next to it. Then the letters:

Dear nephew / Dear Willi / Dear brother in Christ
it is with great sorrow / a delicate / Seifert, a high school teacher
I shall pray / to make matters worse / in your parish
repent of your / Jewish sympathies / and use your influence
you'll have the strength / of a Jew / his confessor
holy mother / a true German / matter quiet

Then he switched his lamp on and called his housekeeper to make some coffee.

Which is just what mother was doing, a few weeks later, in Aschaffenburg, in the new apartment, when

THE THIRD LETTER TOOK SHAPE.

A thin, black shape with a horsey face, long like the sermons that issued from it, with large, yellowed teeth.

"Frau Seifert? Allow me, Father Schneffenhoff, your parish priest."

A guest. Charming Frau Seifert:

"Will you have a cup of coffee? I'm just filtering some."

"Herr Seifert. I just stopped in..."

"Hardly the weather for it, in this rain."

Josef was suspicious. He went to church some Sundays. But housecalls from the priest?

"Oh, I always welcome new members to the parish. You're practicing, I hope?"

"Member."

"?"

"Member. In the singular. My wife's not a Catholic."

"Ah."

Here the heretic wife came in with the steaming pot and one sixteenth of an inch of fresh powder on her face.

"I made it extra strong."

"Thank you, my child."

"Child indeed! A mother of two!"

"I'm sorry, I didn't mean... the customs of our church... The two children, I hope, are...

"Yes, yes. You don't need to worry, they're Catholic alright. It's just me you got to count out."

"What a pity, my ch...*gnädige Frau*. The family that prays together..."

He had very blue eyes and a carefully cultivated stare which he thought of as penetrating.

"Another cup?"

"Well," snorted Frederika afterwards, "what great secret did the pastor have to discuss with his sheep? You look angry."

"That same damn affair."

Frederika bristled:

"How does he know? And what business is it of his?"

"Comes here to 'welcome new parishoners!' Tries to hustle me into his confessional! By express. Tells me I'm in a state of mortal sin. I say: 'What can you mean?'

"'You are slandering a member of the clergy.'

"Then it dawns on me. 'Will you explain yourself, father?'

"He tells me I put a false interpretation on insufficient evidence.

"'Are you telling me what I saw?'

"'What did you see, my son?'

"'Father Schnepfenhopf...'

"'Schneffenhoff.'

"'...Schneffenhoff, you would oblige me by leaving my affairs to myself.'

"Then he starts threatening me with anything from excommunication to god knows what. Nice start, this is. And all because of you."

"*I* didn't drag any priest into this."

Not properly humble, our mother. And still a head taller than her husband.

FATHER DOPPLER FROWNED

as he read the letters from Josef and from Father Schneffenhoff. He wrote another letter: to the Bishop of Würzburg. A long letter. It recalled the time when the Bishop was teaching at the seminary. How well the writer remembered his brilliant lectures, his irrefutable argumentation. It seemed like yesterday. But time flies. He nearly added "in flocks" because his eyes had strayed out the window to the fluttering throng on the telegraph wires. Now and then, one of the swallows shot back at the house, straight like an arrow, then with a little dip down to avoid the roof and straight up to the nests, balls of clay glued below the roof with beadfuls of spittle. He would miss them. It was fall. The migration was starting.

The Bishop returned a severe question. Had the chaplain's case been reported to the Council on Discipline?

Doppler squirmed a little. Knowing that the Bishop was a

member of said council he had thought of taking this perhaps some-
what informal way... But as to the other side of the problem, did the
Bishop not agree that it was a matter of prime importance to keep it an
internal matter? Especially considering the political climate.

The Bishop wrote back: What can be done?

Doppler admitted that Schneffenhoff had been a mistake. The
Bishop knew the staff of the diocese. Perhaps a more diplomatic man?
Maybe the other party could also be contacted. Seifert seemed willing
to settle out of court.

"Herr Seifert, I'd like to speak to you."

"Certainly, Herr Director."

"I have a complaint here from Father Schneffenhoff. Says you
showed him the door. Rather impolite, I'd say."

"Herr Director, he..."

"Seifert, I understand. I have no intention of meddling with your
religion or your lack of it. But you have to keep up the forms. This is
embarrassing for the school. We must cooperate with the churches.
Aschaffenburg is 68 percent Roman Catholic. And then he said you're
accusing some priest of homosexuality..."

"Herr Director, let me..."

"I say, hands off, Seifert. This is explosive stuff. I want no scandal.
Especially not with the church."

Two days later, a man with a camera rang the Seiferts' door bell.

"Herr Professor Seifert? I'm from the *Abendnachrichten*. I'd like
to have a statement from you about the homosexuality at our high
school."

THERE THEY LIE

in their beds. In Aschaffenburg. There are lots of things to hear, in
Aschaffenburg, in Offenbachstrasse, if you are Josef Seifert. If you are
Frederika, you only hear an occasional whimper from one of the twins
and you hear Josef sighing. You get cross and wonder if it is worth
taking your blanket and moving to the couch in the living room.

But if you are Josef, a bare branch of the chestnut tree scrapes
against the house. A winter fly buzzes, lazily. Already. The wood

creaks: it is a new house, not yet settled. And later the wind, Frederika's even breath. Sometimes he thinks he hears a dream glide through it with the slightest murmur of displaced water. Franz? he wonders. His eyes fixed on Bayreuth again. Again. The frame defined. Franz at the piano. Again. The station again. Buff brick and the orchards starting right behind it, apple trees, white, it is spring. Franz and Frederika. Franz and Frederika off to their honeymoon. Franz's hand square on her ass, helping her into the train. Arranged by Josef. A bee strays from the blossoms. He chases it off the babies.

Josef shut his eyes. Sleep did not come to rid him of his night self. Only a cough which he tried to suppress. Not now. Don't let her wake up now.

And the reporter again. The second one. The one who wasn't easily put off.

"A mistake? A different town? Man, you make me laugh. That Yid director doesn't want you to talk. And you knuckle under? You'll regret it if you don't speak out. Or maybe you're with them? A warm brother yourself, maybe? I'm warning you. Us parents won't stand for it. Degenerates debauching our children. What kind of an asslicker are you? What kind of a German? Alright, alright, I'm going. But you'll remember this. Us Germans..."

Here they come. Running. Faces out of the dark. And fingers. Thick white sausage fingers all pointed at him. Here they come, the parents, the German parents. All beaks and claws. They tear at him and pull and tear and tear off his clothes.

Silence. Sudden. Eyes on his prick. Then the howl rises again. Beaks posed to carve. He wants to cry out, but his tongue is swollen, thick, too big in his mouth.

Josef jumped, tore his eyes open, shivering, in a sweat.

"THEN WHO

sent those reporters to me, I'd like to know, Herr Director."

"Seifert, I'd be the last one to attract attention to this. If I wanted to get rid of you there are simpler ways. And much more elegant. This is as annoying to me as to you. More so. *Der Angriff.* What is that anyway, an army sheet? No doubt pan-German and patriotic?"

Josef became frosty:

"You were not in the army, I take it. Or you wouldn't . . ."

"The army! So you're sentimental about the army too. I haven't seen this paper. I don't say it's filth like the *Völkische Beobachter*. But have you ever seen anything connected with the army that wasn't reactionary? Nationalist in the worst, narrowest sense?"

"I must ask you not to make assumptions as to what I'm sentimental about. And I won't have 'national' and 'patriotic' used as if they were dirty words. Besides, I didn't tell either reporter anything."

When Josef got angry he interrupted nearly as well as Director Goldschmidt.

"Well, let's hope you discouraged them both."

The *Aschaffenburger Abendnachrichten* was silent. But

DER ANGRIFF

carried a headline: GERMAN PARENTS PROTECT YOUR CHILDREN. And a sub heading: YOUNG TEACHER SILENCED.

. . . WITNESSED AN ACT OF HOMOSEXUALITY. . . INTIMIDATED. . . DECLARES IT AN "UNFOUNDED RUMOR". . . CORRUPT OUR CHILDREN BEFORE OUR EYES. PROOF HOW JEWS, FREEMASONS AND COMMUNISTS MAKE A RELIGION OF THE LOWEST AND BASEST INSTINCTS. . . RELIGION OF DESTRUCTION. DESTRUCTION OF OUR VALUES, MORALITY, RACE. . . THE HEALTH OF THE NATION. . . PERVERTED ASIATIC SPIRIT . . . GERMAN PARENTS. . . AGAINST JEWISH PERVERSION AND CRIME. . .

"You read that rag?"

"Glanced at it."

"A nest of poison pens."

"Better than a nest of ninnies."

"Can it be true?"

"Where there's smoke . . ."

"Jews involved too."

"Where there's something rotten . . ."
"And priests."
"They always try to drag the church in."

The teachers were assembled in Goldschmidt's office.

"I don't know whom among us we have to thank for this," the director said. I'm not going to point my finger without evidence. I only want you to know this: Number one, the school is going to sue *Der Angriff* for libel. I have recommended that Seifert join or sue on his own account. Number two, it is correct that our colleague Seifert and I had a conversation about a case of homosexuality. But the reference was indeed to a different school. So you can set your minds at rest. I count on you to convey this to any parents who might contact you."

"Perverts let loose on our children."
"And getting paid for it."
"That's right: our money."
"Jews."
"Perverts."
"Bolsheviks."

The teachers were again assembled in Goldschmidt's office.

"The police have been notified. All classes will be dismissed at 2 o'clock, this afternoon. The police will guard the school and access streets today and tomorrow. Longer, if necessary. I don't think there will be any more mud throwing."

Der Angriff put in larger headlines. Longer articles.

THE POLICE OF OUR "DEMOCRATIC" STATE ARE AFRAID TO ARREST CRIMINAL PERVERTS. THIS WE HAVE KNOWN. BUT THEY DO NOT SCRUPLE TO TAKE THEIR BILLY-STICKS TO THE PEOPLE. RIGHTEOUSLY INDIG-NANT PARENTS WHO ASSEMBLED AT THE GYMNASIUM TO DEMONSTRATE FOUND THEMSELVES FACING A POLICE CORDON . . .

"The country's in bad hands."
"Right. No authority."

"They are making a farce out of law and order."
"And a brothel out of the school room."

In Würzburg, in the Episcopal palace:
"It will all be cleared up. Innocence will be vindicated."
"Meanwhile the church is pulled through the gutter."
"Also, you forget that there are interests which do not want us innocent."
"But they'll concentrate on the Jews."

The *Abendnachrichten* and the *Bayernkurier* carried disclaimers. The *Völkische Beobachter* screamed:

WHERE IS THE FREEDOM OF THE PRESS NOW?
COURAGEOUS PAPER UNVEILS CRIMINAL ABUSE IN OUR
"REPUBLIC." WHAT HAPPENS? THE "LIBERAL" COURTS
SCREAM LIBEL. THE "LIBERAL" PRESS TALKS ABOUT
"HUMAN RIGHTS." AND TO WHAT END? ALL IN ORDER
TO GLORIFY CRIME...

It seemed everyone got involved. Just as everybody forgot about it soon after. Some were no doubt prompted by principle, by morality, others by faction, racism, interest, a wish to see heads roll or at least ink flow, to chalk up a score and let it bear interest, to talk about sex, to picture perversion.

"But why me?" cried Josef who, in the space of a few weeks, had been kissed by priests, raped by Jews, had sucked his colleagues, buggered his pupils, fingered cocks, licked assholes, choreographed gangbangs.

Director Goldschmidt and he agreed: he should transfer again. Right away. At the Christmas break. Not even waiting out the year.

AT THE BEGINNING OF THE SCANDAL,

mother had eagerly chatted with the grocer. Had enjoyed her sudden importance:

"No. No. *Wo denken Sie hin*. Not here. It was in Bayreuth. My husband had himself transferred here because he didn't want to be part of it. Such a *Schweinerei*."

As it wore on, she turned against Josef along with public opinion. Even though she knew the accusations to be false he was tainted by them. She was indignant, not against the falsehood, but that it could be connected with her. What kind of morass was Josef leading her into?

Naked bodies come unbidden to mother's bed. Even in her dreams, Frederika draws herself up, battles, a respectable woman, against the throbs of sleep that batter her upright resolve, pull her down where Rome is burning around a sleeping Brünhild.

A spear breaks the ring of fire, comes flying on borrowed strength. The wrong man leaps through the flames.

"What fertile, what arable land," he says.

But Frederika knows the story.

"You can't afford an inch of it," she says to Josef and looks for the invisible strong man behind him, her own Siegfried. Or is it Nero whose fiddle she hears in the distance, off pitch?

"I offer you my heart," Josef says, taking it out of his chest like the Jesus pictures home on the farm. "It is my strongest muscle."

"It takes more than that to get me to the top."

Here, mother wakes as I wake when I have wrested the whip from her, when I am pointing the knife and don't want to know at whom. She wakes with a sense of cocks erect, spread legs and flaming cunts.

Frederika had seen herself, mother of twins, against a luminous backdrop of blue sun and approbation. Her face glowing with its own light. A warm image. Like the duet in *Jesu der du meine Seele* where the organ comes as close to waltzing as you can in 2/2 time. She could also have accepted funeral marches and the black of tragedy. A jewel in a velvet casket. She could have stood nearly anything with the proper ground. But nastiness has no pigment. And if there is no color, how can it match her complexion?

This particular nastiness actually had a pigment. Brown. A perfectly decent color. It can't be blamed for the people that put it on.

It was not a penitent wife who moved to Kitzingen, on the first of January, 1930. Still a head taller than Josef. They were even. At least. He too had fallen down on his promises.

THE ASHTRAY

comes slowly into focus, restoring the present. A glow on a tip of tobacco. Memories knocked off with the pile of ashes, grey over the colors.

Please stop harping on "truth," Andrea. Not for us, not for the little net we cast into the whirl and welter: the past is an imposter. It obeys our expectations. With a bit of seducing, I suppose.

As for the present, why do I put up with your letters? I don't remember telling *you* how to live. We, I mean you and I, should not use words. I should just play the piano for your dance exercises again. Though even then we ended up yelling at one another. Then from ballet school into the convent. Different ways of being on your toes. Always to extremes. Like mother. Like King Ludwig's horse on the Odeonsplatz you pass every day: its left hoof raised for over a hundred years now. I do not have to have studied ballet to know how impossible a posture that is. Here in Providence we are more sedate. General Burnside's horse has all four legs planted solidly on the pedestal. And the field glasses—this general is not going to strain his eyes by a century's long focus—he only holds them, casually, in his right hand.

It is foggy out. I can barely see across the street. But on the left, the grey house looms up. Foggy as hearing bells from a great distance, as breaking down the door and seeing mother in bed, pointing the carving knife at us. At father, that is. And the silence so thick you could cut it. With her knife. Andrea, you don't know what nerve you touched when you said: "Tell me what happened with the knife. Try to remember." I have no qualms about imagining mother in all sorts of scenes, lending her motives, lines. But here I can't. Here I am frozen. Here I am a powerless idiot. Yes, I see it all clearly. You can ask me what she wore: her brown velvet evening dress with the braided gold belt. But then the fog closes in again and I do not know how it was— what? Resolved? Nothing was ever resolved. How it all kept muddling along till the next crisis lit up a scene and burned it into my memory.

All I can say is that sometimes a single image, like mother with the knife, becomes the key to a whole chain of events. It made visible her power to destroy. Though there was no murder in the family. No suicide either. No funeral with flowers and black suits, with red eyes and oh the poor children. With: well, he can't be all innocent, must have driven her to it.

No. Instead, the usual bustle. By the clock. Frederika née Wolgamot cooked and cleaned and sewed and saved and washed and
worked and could not be asked any questions.

The widow's walk on the grey house has come out of the fog. Pity
our house does not have one too. I could look for Bob in this fog the way
they used to look out for ship ahoy or not a speck on the horizon. Before
the harbor was filled in and made into downtown Providence. Before
chain hoists and anchors gave way to the three-piece-suits going in and
out of Rhode Island Hopital Trust and The Old Stone Bank. Before the
Rhode Runner buses started cruising where the waves had lapped
against rotting pilings. I could stand up there on the widow's walk,
hands on the railing. And maybe I would see him joining a thin figure
with shoulders just slightly hunched as if she were chilly. And tonight
she would be. Would I hold on to the railing or let it go lightly, like a
keyboard? No. We are sober here, in Providence. Even if Bob put his
arm around this figure with his very own kind of hesitancy and led her
into the house. Maybe my knuckles would turn white. In the fog you
couldn't tell anyway.

Unlike the flute or violin, the piano does not sustain its vibrations,
does not continue to feed energy into them. The original impact of the
hammer must do. The vibrations are "free," and depend on how the
energy in the string is dissipated along Elmgrove and Elton or, if the
wind carries it to the other side, as far as Humboldt or even Angell
Streets.

KITZINGEN ON THE MAIN.

It was not quite *my* Kitzingen yet. In *my* Kitzingen everybody got
along fine with everybody else. Everybody spoke the proper language
properly, the dialect of the region. Everybody talked. Everybody listened. No: nobody listened. Everybody whispered, mouth to ear and a
hand cupped around it.

They were solid. They held down their jobs with their heavy
haunches. They stood up for their rights on properly soled shoes.

Mayor Korbach pulled the town through the difficult years. The
post-war years. Now he had a street named after him. Everybody got
on in years. On market day, the farmers came in with their eggs and
chicken and vegetables in carts. The superintendent of schools, our
own Karl, our brother-in-law, was sad that the women were not wear-

ing the large skirts any more, like Aunt Margaret, the full ones, three or four petticoats one over the other, broad as the dome of St. Peter's. Or nearly. Even so, he liked to talk to them. Then he could go home and tell Doria how happy, how contented they are.

"The simple life," he said.

The industry of the town was blooming and booming. A system of expressways was under construction. Businesses sprang up and dissolved. Doctors were licenced and consulted. The prison was enlarged, new schools were needed and teachers still respected, to Karl's relief. Even the young redhead. Though the natives said he won't get anywhere with that funny name of his: Witkocewicz. From Lithuania or somewhere. On Christmas there were Christmas trees all over town. And parsons, one for each denomination. The kids advanced from one grade to the next or not. And occasionally somebody stepped on somebody's toes. With well-soled shoes.

HAPHAZARD PLACE: KITZINGEN.

The whole town has a haphazard air. With the "Schiefe Turm," its tower off kilter. With its crooked streets and houses as if assembled from a set of building blocks. Even though we know there are venerable bits of the city wall left from the eighth century, their origin was haphazard: A hanky dropped from a window of castle Schwanberg by the daughter of Pippin the Short. The one action out of her whole life to enter history, well, *local* history. Note that her name didn't make it in. She is just Pippin's daughter. But the wind carried the bit of cloth down the mountain side, played with it, tossed it up, flouting superior strength, and then unclenched its grip, letting the lacy butterfly sag and fall. Down by the river, the Main, shepherd Kitz found it crumpled and soggy with dew. The town of Kitzingen was built on the spot. And if it weren't for the weight of the churches, the handkerchief might even now rise up again on a fillip of wind, and the whole town wander off with it, farther up the river.

Our garbage man here, in Providence, is named Pippin. *Sic transit gloria*. And the castle is an old folks home now. But maybe the decline isn't such a long way. As I knew in the first grade:

Pippin der Kleine
hat beschissne Beine.

Let it be said, however, that if he beshit his legs, he did it for the sake of rhyme. If he had been Pippin the Great he would have had other choices. Unlike his daughter who had no choice at all, with her one gesture, stuck at her window, forever dropping her one hanky for a shepherd seven miles away. Without so much as her name entering the legend. Or Josef's mother with her one action, slapping her child. With her not so soft hand.

And now there is Frederika, our mother, at that castle window. "Old Folks Home Schwanberg." Still regretting the voice lessons her father refused.

FREDERIKA WAS NOT PENITENT.

She neither bathed Josef's feet in tears nor dried them with her hair. Though Josef wanted to sling her lover's corpse around her neck and watch her go weighted down through the days. A dead weight is a good deal heavier than any other. And Kitzingen (mine as well as theirs) would have approved. It's not proper in Kitzingen that the wife be a head taller than the husband. A humbler posture might have corrected the matter. But mother had gone and buried her affection. Angrily. Under more than the necessary amount of earth. Her lover could be forgotten.

YOU ARE THE ONE

who did penance, Andrea. You were determined to wrench out of yourself anything that might make for a coat of a different color from the Carmelite habit. The violence of it. Like mother's. Yes, like mother's even though the direction seemed Josef's, the world of the spirit. But always to extremes. That you had to choose the Carmel. Though I also admired you for it, for the recklessness, the glitter of the absolute. Denying anything you had ever loved. Like talking. It came hard. For days you had to wear a piece of wood across your mouth: BROKE THE RULE OF SILENCE.

The barrenness you had let yourself in for. Worse than being evicted in the middle of a Minnesota winter. You had to throw fits again. Fits of silence this time. Not like the convulsions you had in order to get away from mother, but equally violent. Why should devotional texts be exempt as long as there was a ban on words? You stood at the lectern of the refectory. Silent. But not like mother: without power. Not using the silence for your designs, as a dramatic moment, as Beethoven does, but locked into it. Helpless, as if it were still mother's silence rather than your own. The spaces between the words grew larger and larger. The page visible like bone beneath the skin. It would have taken—what? A throat cleared of the memory of books and streets, hankering for no words but those on the page. But now it swallowed back what your lips formed, as through the wrong end of a megaphone.

"It was terrible," you said. "How to explain it. Explain it away."

FREDERIKA DID NOT EXPLAIN.

She did not bow her head. She stood on tiptoe to peer at what might be coming her way. Flung herself wildly, like a whirlwind, into the fissures and caverns of the new town. Cyclones are likely to originate when the doldrums lie at their greatest distance from the equator, where the rotational deflexion is considerable. Charming Frau Seifert. A frenzy to fill the space that might be herself. The space where the cock crows, the dancers fade away, the music stops, an immense spread chord fading into silence.

This cannot be faced. Better to spank her children just to feel her hand against a solid obstacle. Her soft hand. Nearly indecent so soft. Better to order them to stand up and sit down and know by their obedience that she exists. Better to laugh up swarms of butterflies, light as the hanky of Pippin's daughter, of which I don't even know if it was dropped by accident or as a signal, a signal of love or of distress, for shepherd Kitz or someone else. Did it carry a message in its folds or only the future of a small town, Kitzingen?

EVERY DAY,

morning rises up from the fields with the river mist. The senses fill up with the certainty of the instant. The clocks are wound. Order is established in Kaltenheimstrasse where I'll learn to crawl but which I don't remember. Then why bring it up? To make clear where we are. A bit outside town. A house with small rooms. Small enough to fall out of sight the moment Josef mounts his bicycle to ride to school, past St. Kilian's fountain. He sits very upright on his saddle as if it were one of our straight-backed chairs. Only his legs move in small circles which roll distance along the street. Not even the wind makes him lean into it. Upright, my father. Maybe yours.

I'll be three when we move again. Move to Moltkestrasse 5. The broken glass of November 1938 had been one large crystal ball in which "Eduard Grossman: Wein und Spirituosen," read the future without the aid of a gypsy. Frau Enck got a bargain and four floors ready to rent out.

I remember dark purple wall paper and:

"I don't want to go in there. It's dark."

"The kid's got instinct. Doesn't want to go into the Jew place."

BUT IT IS ONLY 1930.

You have only just moved to Kitzingen. Now we start all over again. Sampling the shops. Meeting the milkman. School parties and charming Frau Seifert. Taking the twins out with harness and leash. The hope of discovery, like a new dress, bright, stiff, not yet tried on. And acquaintances to court with a profusion of little attentions, presents, invitations. Total conquest. Tomorrow the world. The course not without variations, but always with the stress on the beginning, while Josef strains for what might be whispered between phrases. He fears to overhear a "take me" spoken softly behind other words, softly, but crashing to his inner ear. His center of balance reels in anticipation, and he grabs for the end of the sentence to make sure, yet hopes that it's a true German sentence and the end a long way off.

I am looking at a childhood photo, the one where you and Doria flank mother in front of—what is the name of that little castle sitting in its moat? Mespelbrunn? You must be lying on your bellies on a hill. Mother propped on her elbows, smiles at the camera. A woman expecting the attention of strangers, the obedience of doors. Father talked about this photo a lot. I remember it in a frame with two Raphael putti pasted underneath. In the same position as you twins.

"What nice quiet children," said Frau Schaderer who always knew where the shoe pinched, where the dog was buried, where the elbow chafed.

"That's what you think. Two of them. They egg each other on. Why, just yesterday I caught them throwing the dishes out of the window. Can you imagine?"

"What's curious about that," father put in, "is that they are at exactly the same age as the young Goethe when he did the same thing."

"Sure, sure," guffawed Herr Schaderer with the full resonance of all his embonpoint. "A sign of genius, no doubt about it."

"That's not what I meant at all," frowned father. "I mean that all children will have the same impulses at the same age—for example to find out what sound a cup makes when it smashes. Only, it isn't usually recorded. I mean the eternal recurrence of even the smallest, seemingly trivial things, the causal nexus of the microcosm. The circular movement of history. Time closes in on itself and becomes substance."

They were sitting around remains of aspic (mother's pride) under the lamp whose six brass arms grew dark spokes over the ceiling and beyond, into the dark outside which wheels around the earth.

"Look at this picture," father went on. "Simple snapshot I took of Frederika and the girls. Yes, it's Mespelbrunn in the background. But notice the positions of the twins, the way they are lying in the grass, one with her left elbow propped on the ground and her chin in her hand, the other resting her head sideways flat on her arm. Mirror answering mirror. Now I'll show you something interesting, the identical configuration, just a moment . . ."

"What really got me," mother picked up her own thread, "wasn't the dishes. I don't keep the good china where they can get at it. But I was splitting the calf's head for this aspic and God knows I have my hands full with all the work to be done—"

"You didn't really do it from scratch?" Frau Hiesiger leaned forward on her chair.

"Always. It isn't nearly as good with gelatine."

"Don't interrupt," Herr Hiesiger minded with the newspaper man's regard for a story, "we were getting to the climax."

"Yes. Suddenly this . . . like a gunshot. I was so startled I dropped the cleaver. Just barely missed my foot. I thought, you know, with all the news, I thought it was guns."

"In Kitzingen?"

"Well, the way things are going you really expect it, don't you?"

"I guess so. Except we're lucky, no heavy industry here. The metal workers were on strike last week. Can you imagine 150,000 men on strike in Berlin alone? I'm glad I'm not in business."

"I tell you, it can't go on like this. It's got to stop."

Frau Schaderer had a tiny bone caught between her teeth and disappeared behind her napkin to fish for it.

"The Hitler people have 107 seats now. Up from 12."

When Josef came back with the Raphael volume to show the two putti flanking the madonna he could not get any attention.

"Brüning can't last, that's for sure."

"If it weren't for the communists, the socialists wouldn't put up with him."

"Five hundred thousand members in that NSDAP."

"Bit scary, isn't it."

"I don't know, at least—"

"Shh... Isn't that your kids calling?"

"They have no business but to be asleep."

"Maybe they're scared by all the voices..."

"*I* am the mother..."

"That's right, don't spoil them."

"Well excuse me, I didn't mean to—"

"What was that you were saying about the army? They're already in there? The Hitler people? Same with the police, it seems. Can't get hired unless you're NSDAP."

Frau Hiesiger leaned forward: "Well, I must admire you. I've never been able to start my aspic from a calf's head. Eek, with the eye staring at you."

"The butcher takes that out."

"That's just as bad. An empty socket."

Then the men disappeared into the study to play cards. Father determined to frame your photograph together with the Raffael putti.

NO PERFORMANCE.

Microtonal slides. Or the two chords between the first and second movements of the Third Brandenburg Concerto. To play them with great feeling and exquisite tone as if they by themselves constituted a whole movement is as absurd as to try to pronounce a comma. Only the clock moves, ticks out your strict routine of sleeping time, feeding time, potty time, nap time, play time, walk time, all leading to further time, like an endless street, yet definite and full. A little grey, the clear daylight on the machinery, ropes and cables. Mother, impatient for the conductor to lift his baton, for the spectacle to resume, be it with another scandal. She cannot lose herself, like Josef, in a polyphony of astral space and bravura flights of the mind.

Frederika and Josef. Acute angles and ectoplasm. Her presence piercing, his foggy. Too much resistance and too little. The notes scatter frantically through the ever widening interval.

LEGAL COMMUNICATIONS.

The libel suit against *Der Angriff* is still dragging on. His honor. Then: State of Bavaria versus civil servants Huber, Franz, and Seifert, Josef. Division of *Beamtenrecht*, disciplinary section.

What good does this do Josef? Now he's right where he started. Worse off. Not a private suit. Not Judge Hatzfeld, but not Judge Kessler either. The mess Father Doppler had got him into: for nothing.

PRELIMINARY HEARING. DISTRICT COURT. WÜRZBURG, MAY 18, 1930.

Würzburg is a beautiful city. But today Josef was blind to the imposing Juliusstrasse, to the baroque facades, the cupola of the Schönbrunn chapel or the castle up on the hill. Nor did he notice, and this is stranger yet, the budding trees along the sidewalks. As little as he had seen the factory signs between Rottendorf and the main station, even though he had looked out of the train window the whole trip. The whole half hour. While the diminishing distance from Würzburg could have been measured quite accurately by the growing contraction at the pit of his stomach.

There they were. Josef and Frederika on one side, Franz on the other, shadowed by their lawyers in their black robes, the secretary in his black robe, the typist in his black robe, two policemen in their blue uniforms, the photographer in his trenchcoat. Now Judge Eckert entered in his black robe with Prosecutor Hoehn in his black robe and with a face as long as a lawsuit itself.

Otherwise the hall was brown, and all I mean here is: of wood. Even Judge Eckert's face seemed cut in wood as he looked at his folder and signaled to Hoehn. Hoehn said: State of Bavaria versus *Beamte* Huber, Franz, and Seifert, Josef. He said: Immoral conduct. He said: Attempt at blackmail. He said: Witnesses.

There were no witnesses. So he said: Exhibit number one. And he read the famous contract of which we know the import, but not the details.

I am rehearsing *Pierrot Lunaire*. I am struck how "Nacht" is drawn entirely from a 3-note-motif, the way we both are trying to construct this story from the two or three meager facts we know. Only the pattern is clearer in Schoenberg, his transpositions, inversions, retrogrades, the E, G, E-flat as melody, or built up into a chord. But there, as in our story, all grows into contrapuntal ramifications which it is hard to believe came out of such simple material and which, by the end, have pushed alarming pockets into the tonal and moral systems.

Had Josef endorsed this contract from misguided chivalry toward his wife? Blind proceeding? The dense fog that results when warm, saturated air blows over a cold surface such as an ice field? Or had he hoped it might still be made to work? Greed? A useful word. Make Franz pay for the resentment he felt?

Years later, when I attacked his double standard in sexual matters, he shook his head: "It's not the same thing. When the woman does it, there is the cuckoo's egg."

"Not blackmail," he said now, after quieting down mother who had jumped up with "Herr Judge, now you listen to me, I am an honest woman—" at which the judge smiled, and the prosecutor wondered why this woman would take up with a Jew, and not even a very handsome one.

"Not blackmail," Josef said. "Alimony. Damages. A contribution to the rearing of the twins as is only fair."

The secretary wrote it all down.

Yes, the mother was certain that Franz Huber was the father. She blushed becomingly as she was pressed for details.

She performed. I can see her leap on her horse. A coquettish circus horse with polished hoofs and grey dapples painted on in just the right intervals. Bareback she sat and began the paces. She had reason to assume. The horse kicked up the sand of the ring. The judge would carry some home in his pocket and, taking off his shoes, would suddenly think of the beach. Differences with her husband. Frederika cantered and felt it to the tips of the feathers on her hat.

No. Josef Seifert did not wish to change the legal status of the twins. The stigma of illegitimacy. Why make the children suffer?

Franz Huber, however, of the magnetic eyes. Yes, he admitted. His complexion still red from the fever within him. But no, he did not think he was the father. Not necessarily. Why not? We wait for the hypnotist's gesture which makes the eyes roll up in their sockets. But he simply said:

"I was not the only lover."

Breaths were drawn in sharply. Josef got up. Frederika's horse reared and whinnied. The bell demanded silence.

Witnesses?

No.

Names?

This he will leave to Frau Seifert.

Frederika rose. She stood on toe, indignantly, and did a little outraged entrechat right there on horseback. She, the shyest, the most innocent of women until seduced by the hypnotic power of. In whom she had confided. She had been invited to a car ride by an acquaintance she would prefer not to name. Said acquaintance, after a pleasant spin, stopped the car on a deserted road and—she blushed again—tried to pull down her panty. But she, the most modest of women, pulled her coat tight and defended her honor. She, the most trusting—here the horse went down on his knees, showing Frederika perched on the most alarming slope—asked Herr Huber's advice on how to treat this acquaintance in the future. Who would have thought—a little tear stole into her eye and glittered more brightly than the rhinestones on her circus leotards—who would have thought he would misuse her confidence to slander her in public when nothing, but nothing at all had happened.

It lacked little and a band would have appeared in the balcony, broken into a flourish, and Frederika alighted from her horse to the thunderous applause of the whole circus tent.

There were frowns in Huber's direction. Clearly no gentleman. What can you expect from a Jew.

Did Herr Huber have something to add?

He did not. Unless you count a little twitch at the corners of the mouth.

FACTS, YOU SAY, ANDREA.

Yes, but you have to be generous with facts. You have to allow what surrounds them, what gives them color and weight. And when you have only bare scraps, a few notes on a piano which, as you know, is of all instruments the most deficient in overtones, then you have to mingle louder and softer timbres in a chord, add horse and circus, to give the utmost play to the harmonics while guiding the ear by a slight emphasis on the leading tones.

You wanted a story. Something with form, like a sonata: beginning, development and resolution. Where one thing would lead to another. Of course, it's my own fault that I tried to comply. I was carried—and deceived—by your version. It seemed easy, or at least possible, to give a different interpretation, to fill gaps, to look at it from another angle. Now, as the paragraphs wear on, I wonder if it is too late to give up the desire to control, to shape a story, and just let things surface as they may.

FREDERIKA LOVED THE CAFÉ LUDWIG

from the moment her image moved through the mirror in the hall, as always in its ornate frame, the gold paint flaking the tiniest bit. The small marble tables, the Biedermeier chairs, the large windows with the net curtains to catch what drifts by in the street.

SHE WAS HAPPY WITH HER PERFORMANCE.

"I told *him*. Trying to make me out a whore."

But Josef was thoughtful. Not happy with the findings. Or the verdict.

"My honor," he thought. "My honor." And did not even notice that Frederika ordered *two* pieces of Schwarzwälder Kirschtorte, a specialty of the house. This time, this one time he was not rendered speechless by such extravagance because he kept repeating to himself:

"...have both conducted themselves in a manner inconsistent with...pulled at my panty...with the dignity of their office...confided in Herr Huber...and the proper discharge of their duties... unprepared because he had not tried to kiss me...as employees of the

State of Bavaria... just barely touched me... in a manner bordering on blackmail... pulled my coat tight... to impose a most questionable... my panty... contract... no woman had ever resisted this much... which violates our standards of moral behavior... probation and a fine of... "

I HAVE MY OWN IDEA

about the car and panty story, though I can even imagine that "nothing, but nothing at all" happened.

Frederika with red cheeks, wind-blown hair. An open coupe. Excited. Daring him to go faster.

"I'm already going 60."

Along the river. Only in a remote way, along the periphery, does Frederika take in the luscious green, the trees along the road as dark verticals whooshing by. The river, moving lazily, reeds, water biting into wet sand.

"Let's stop at the Waldcafé," Frederika suggested.

"I know a better place."

"But I'm hungry."

"The other place isn't far."

"But I *want* to stop at the Waldcafé."

"Half of Bayreuth's going to be there."

"That's fine with me."

Frederika would like to be seen by half of Bayreuth. This half. The half with cars. And villas. The riding club half. But he drives on.

"You'll like this one. You'll be surprised."

Frederika is not sure. Gets sullen, silent as they drive on.

Up a woody hill. Stop. As the man holds the door open for her he notices, as she swings her legs out in a carefully casual movement which she has been rehearsing in her mind for the last half hour, notices her thighs opening as one foot reaches the ground, notices, as her dress slides back, notices tht she is naked underneath. And Frederika looking him full in the face.

The restaurant is charming. They sit on the terrace looking down a green slope. The man watches Frederika eat. Gluttonously. No polite remains on her plate. The food's too delicious. Ragout fin. It revives the man's appetite just to watch her. But Frederika does not like it. There is nobody here. Nobody to see her get out of the car as if she were used to it.

After the meal, the man suggests they take a walk, but Frederika wants to be back in the car, back by the river, the open spaces, she doesn't like the woods.

The man is puzzled. He stops the car soon and slides his hand up her thigh. He is shocked to get his hand slapped. To get nowhere. After all this.

Childish revenge on my part? The mother seen as always punishing? By the way, do you think it is possible that I was not named after St. Lucy, but after the Lusitania?

Frozen moments. Too clear and too fuzzy at the same time. The focus on one detail which sticks out too brightly, the curl showing every single hair, the dress its weave, the skin its moles and enlarged pores. All the rest is blurred and fades into the surroundings. But perhaps it is this indistinctness that keeps me thinking about them. Perhaps it is these shadowy areas which make a person, not the clear patches we call qualities or traits of character.

FREDERIKA LOVED THE CAFÉ LUDWIG.

"Nearly like the Kranzler," she sighed. "At least Würzburg is a city. If we could live *here* ... "

This pulled Josef out of his phrases. Or had the coffee, good and strong, sharpened his hearing?

"Live here! I'll have to appeal this verdict. God knows what it'll cost—and all you can think of is fantasies like 'live here!'"

Night and day are more than a turn of phrase, she thought. And: It is a good thing that the torte is good. A whole pastry bar. The line of zinc about marks the height of her navel.

A city. Tall buildings and shops. Three dress shops within this block alone. Elegant. And the women in the street. Gives you ideas. A body needs to be dressed. Josef would have agreed: The body is a wound.

THAT NIGHT

which, as usual, came down the Schwanberg and slowly along the Main, there were already a few frogs on the banks swearing they'd sing like nightingales, and an occasional, still timid cricket. You twins had calmed down into sleep after your unusual day with a babysitter. A smoldering took shape. Isolation of a flare.

"Who was it?"

"What?"

"The man with the car."

"Oh. Dr. Eichler."

"The swine. Why didn't you tell *me*?"

"You'd have made a scene."

"For good reason."

"I can defend myself."

"When you want to . . . Who else?"

He knew this was a mistake even as he said it.

IV

YES, ANDREA,

it has been a while since the last comment of Bob's. It was hard to get used to the house without Laff. Now it is without Bob also. Empty. No body to sound against. I imagine my scales pursuing him. I listen for footsteps in the rests which grow longer and longer. I've watched two friends throw themselves into "flurries of women" when their wives left. "I was transparent," said Ken, "I didn't exist unless I fucked." And you seemed to feel this way too when Jesus would not have you as his "bride." One doesn't have the heart to stay out in the dark, under the cold sky, when one is locked out of one's house. One runs for the next row of lit-up windows where people sit down to eat, children scream, lovers laugh and lie down in their beds. One runs where shops stream light on the crowds of shoppers, where cars and buses dash through the streets, and the movie doors swing open on the expectation of pleasure.

I can play it through in my mind too, opening my cunt to the four winds. But I don't think it is for me. Not resignation either, let alone renunciation, that thing you read about in novels or are told about some great-grand-aunt. Though I'm closer to understanding it: as if an intense feeling could tear open our cultural pocket and tumble us into strange latitudes. You tried it. Renunciation. And tumbled back. When the temperature is below freezing the fog deposit forms dazzlingly white rime which can attain remarkable dimensions, growing out with a sharp edge to windward. Its weight may break slender poles and telegraph wires.

117

If I were at least sick, instead of just sitting here and trying to imagine where Bob is and what he is doing now or, rather, trying to keep my mind from returning to this one groove... Oh, never mind. But I now realize that I have conducted a series of tests on the relation of Bob and Lucy Harris. While the tests were going on, while Laff was around, the situation in itself became stable and its purpose obscure. Now that Laff's departure has upset the balance, I know, I just know, Bob is also leaving for good. There is no stopping rust.

After all, the norm is not success, the lasting marriage, the perfect blend of happiness, tone color, degree of legato and evenness of playing, but failure, loss, divorce, error. So I sit here, holding on to my pain as to some last strawberry shortcake, and haven't even opened the Mumma score, though rehearsals are about to start.

I HAD A DREAM.

I sat in mother's bed again. In her brown dress with the braided gold belt. I was holding the knife, her kitchen knife, but there was nobody to point it at. I finally stabbed myself. My lungs rose from my chest and, like punctured balloons, shriveled and jetted a crazy course into the air. Then I tossed the memory of air in my head and could not recall the process of oxidation.

BUT WHAT HAPPENED INDEED

between 1930 and "the kid's got instinct, doesn't want to go into the Jew place." Swastika caramels and Goering dolls. Torchlight processions. GERMAN PEOPLE, DEFEND YOURSELF: DON'T BUY FROM THE JEW. SA marches. *Winterhilfswerk* and *Kraft durch Freude*. Maybe nothing happened. Maybe it had always been: Franz is alright *even though* he's Jewish.

Do you need me to tell you of the day in 1931 when the streets were strangely empty? People were queuing at the bank the way they had been at the baker's and butcher's. Unnaturally silent. Tense as in the days preceding the war. Woe to the kid whose ball rolled on one of the feet in that line.

"Our savings!"

"Again."

"It's the French."

"The Jews."

"And more taxes."

"What do they think a body can live on? One potato a week?"

Do you need me to tell you of queues? And rationing? It did not help the quarrels at home, the vague storm that was always in the air. Tooth and tongue. And nail.

I recall the feeling from later years: the charge in the air spoke to my skin. Goosepimples, cautious breathing. A sharp, unfriendly sound from the kitchen denies even the possibility of music. Mother vigilant against breaks in her pattern. The spoon to be washed before the knife, the batter stirred clockwise. But father is obstinate if quiet, his desire hostile. A word charges like a mad bull across the pasture. The fence shatters. Blood spurts over the sky.

Josef and Frederika tear into each other, carve away. They've never gone deep enough. Always willing to go deeper still. Then the tension flags, the bull prepares to eat a dandelion, and the temperature has gone down. A last growl:

"Why do you always have to pick Sunday to fight? Just like nazis and commies."

DO YOU NEED ME TO REMIND YOU THAT THE NAZIS GAINED VOTES?

"They'll be in with the next election."

"They'll get the country on its feet again. Strong government, that's what we need."

"But they're hoods."

"Don't be a child. Anybody in power takes care of his enemies. And at least they're on the side of the little man, for a change. Not Barons and Junkers. Socialists."

"You forget the National. It comes before Socialist."

"What's wrong with National? Better than the commies."

Outside the story, all the sentences are possible, whereas inside, a "then" brings out unexpected threads and lines of force. But there are obvious holes where all that escapes the story looks on. These holes eventually show through. More and more, here, unnerving me. The words land, without warning, among cries and Siegheils.

THEN FALL

with its depressions and cold fronts. Rain. Rain. Rain. The earth soft underfoot. The valley seemed to sink deeper with every step. Only the birds sit high up in the air as if it were a solid perch. Those that don't migrate, that is. Sparrows. Chickadees.

JOSEF WROTE APPEALS

to the ministry. I decline any compensation. I demand my right. My honor. Waited for answers. Studied law books. Waited. Studied some more. Got impatient. Got resentful. The *ewig-weibliche!* It had more than fallen short of pulling him upward. Had it not been just at the moment when he was about to scale the heights, the steep gradient—no, not just in his career, but in his spiritual progress? Had he not been at this crucial point when the trouble with Frederika began to sap his energies and cloud his aura with negative emotion?

To think that Franz had been with him in the plane when the dizzying height had first given him the sense of *aethrobacy,* of levitation, the earth shrinking and sinking, reduced gravity, reversed polarization. O Wotan, give me thy breath. Earth, let me loose that I may rise. A winging polyphony of bodies within his material one, finer, yearning to rise higher still and unite with the blinding new light, the ethereal essence. A mixture of pride and modesty had held the words back in his throat. But it had not hindered their rising up into his brain where they opened out vistas beyond what you could see from the top of the leaning tower of Kitzingen, the "Schiefe Turm." Vistas not hemmed in by gentle hills, like the Schwanberg, which with their luscious green disguise the fact that they are confining you. Vistas of sky glowing with a pure passion where the known snaps like a paper ribbon, irrelevant. But his wings were clipped, his energies sapped.

was too simple, too uneducated to be aware of his sacrifice, to measure its magnitude. "A heart unfortified, a mind impatient, an understanding simple and unschooled." She had never been tempted by the curve of the eagle's flight.

Frederika nursed the same kind of bitterness: Her voice! Her ambitions brushed aside, first by her father, then her husband. Men! The pitch once struck turns into a drone. The church choir! When she needed curtain calls and bouquets of roses. If she had not married Josef, had not given him and the children her best years. Or if she had married a man who properly valued her gifts and whose funds did not give out.

"Why didn't you take singing lessons when you had a job in Berlin?"

"On my small salary?"

Or if at least they could join the country club. Play tennis. Dip balls into the warm air in immaculate white shorts.

YES, ANDREA. I ADMIT IT:
I WANT TO DAMN HER TOO.

We both have the killer spirit. When I take her knife in my dream I mean to strike. When I take the pen I mean to damn her, though not for a lover or two, but for her pulp desires. We're an unforgiving lot, the two of us. Doria is different. Doria has come to terms with her, in spite of mother freezing her sex. A vaulted belly teaches you patience, I suppose, revokes revenge. Gestation maps into the past as into the future. I think the birth of Doria's first child also marked the birth of her new mother—who did not stand rigid in the middle of the kitchen, her eye on the clock, but with whom the air flowed freely and prolonged the song. But even now, I'm still pretending: it's not mother's frivolities. Surely I could forgive her those. It's her silence. Snow queen and stony goddess. Not a rhythmic breathing as in Couperin or even Beethoven's dramatic moments. The determining factor of the design. To hinder growth of any kind. If there is blood let it freeze.

JOSEF JOINED THE PARTY.

The NSDAP: National Socialist German Worker's Party. Because, as we all know, in 1933 everybody had to join if he wanted to keep his job.

Only, he did not join in 1933, after the deal, after the fire, after the emergency laws. He joined a little earlier. 1932.

A sense of which way the exhaust was blowing? Resentment at his appeals getting nowhere? Taken in by the "little man" talk? Fascinated by the man, by Hitler? Andrea, if you keep pestering me I'll say Josef fell for Hitler because he campaigned by airplane. That will fix you. It will be on the level of your claiming that mother was sexually attracted by Hitler.

I have been very upset by this fantasy of yours, her going back to the movie again and again, to see "his look like lightning." I say "fantasy"—defending myself against the complicity you force on me. The worst is: it rings true to me. I too remember the way she said: "Our leader." Fervently. But it could not have been

HIS VOICE,

loud as it was. From the radio, which was black, taller than wide, small, two knobs framing a dial toward the bottom. A round area of golden-brown cloth where I poked my finger when nobody was looking. Golden-brown. With the golden-brown voice coming out of it. Not the kind of voice that fills the hollows of your body. This one crisped your muscles till you thought you couldn't stand it. *"The Germans are the greatest people on earth. It is not your fault that you were defeated in the war and have suffered so much since. It is because you were betrayed in 1918..."* Piercing like garlic, like a revival preacher's. Modulating from sneering to unctious, from hysterics to fury. A good sixth above normal speaking level, still going up. *"And have been exploited ever since by those who are envious of you..."* Voice on the point of breaking. *"...and hate you..."* Up and up. And breaking. A crack, a kind of slur, a moment of nothing. And the next words a hoarse growl, lower, but rising again, fast, hoarsely. *"...hate you because you've been honest, too honest and too patient. Let Germany awaken and renew her strength, let her remember her greatness and recover her old position in the world."*

"He really can talk, " said Josef and poured another beer. On the Marktplatz where the speeches were broadcast, where the black-white-red flag rolled from the townhall balcony, the crowd was hushed as in church. And when evening came and the torchlight procession marched through town people said:
"Isn't this beautiful."

NOT THE VOICE.

Andrea, I'm your most willing accomplice. I like your description: "Her knees gave way, her clothes suddenly seemed too large, but her eyes dilated and voraciously returned his look — 'like fire' — though it was only directed at the camera." The better to damn her. Yes. And of course, Hitler patting children on the head. If only she could have been there with you, with twins.

And now that we have gotten Frederika bursting with expectations and so wet with enthusiasm that she would have died for this man — what is a life anyway that is not lived on a knife-blade, cutting into the unknown — now that we let her go home and change her famous panty, shall we two go on with our little tricks? We two, Andrea. Shall we play a game of, say,

ADAM AND EVE?

Josef had always thought of politics as a playing on forces which the politician himself is not likely to understand. Interactions. Electrical currents. Cycles. Oscillations of the constant givens — if not, what an abyss. Frederika's enthusiasm. A force emanating from this man. Josef did not know our theory: that she felt him entirely, sexually, inside her, boots, belt and buckle. Metallic. Hard. Impossible to dislodge or digest. That she felt her muscles obey him, her arm go up to pluck the apple of the salute all by itself. Our leader. Josef trusted intuition. Only, in these decadent and corrupt times, with our psychic forces dried and withered, who was in touch with the real forces that shape a nation's destiny? Who could say? If this man should be able to tap them, harness them...

Frederika, he had to admit, had intuitions, had sometimes come close to second sight. Never mind that the sky hardens when she looks at it. Never mind the torrent of words from Berlin and Bayreuth to Aschaffenburg to Kitzingen and back. The flood of grievances. The day you. The times you. How often you. Although you. Never mind. Maybe she had her finger on the crossing of powers which he was trying to map in his twofold awareness. Matter and spirit. Ethereal doubles. Ah, our blind fumbling, our inability to accept, to act in accordance with, the larger forces. Maybe genius came out of this—but at what cost. And if you thought of a whole people what could result but disaster. Too large a unit to assert a spiritual destiny against the grain and pay for it with personal misery. Whereas a leader in the true sense, a conductor of these ungraspable currents, magnetic, other... It would not be right to sit back while he hauled stones. But if he could not handle it? Was not pure enough? Lack of adaptation on a deeper, more dangerous level? Adversary mightier than all the nations of Europe, Asia and America. He would unchain chaos.

So Josef listened to the hysterical promises: *"If the economic experts say this or that is impossible, to hell with economics. What counts is will, and if our will is hard and ruthless enough we can do anything."* He wondered. If one could trust Hitler. Believe in him. What an immense relief, giving yourself up to someone larger, stronger. Being a muscle, a mere fibre of a muscle in a larger body, an atom of a larger force.

YOU OUGHT TO UNDERSTAND THIS, ANDREA.

You had the same temptation to be an atom inside your boxes of convent, church, community of saints. Walls and walls and hierarchies. The temptation, the excuse of obedience. As long as you obeyed your superior you could not commit any fault. You would go to heaven as if in your sleep. "Obedience, O sovereign liberty," exclaimed St. Jerome. "O holy and blessed security." With you, mother fought it and knew what she was fighting. Elsewhere, she did not see as clearly. But your ship was at the most delayed by head winds. It would have withstood the Roaring Forties and Wild Westerlies.

And even now you're still following the outdated sailing course of Catholicism: They would not have you as a saint? They'll have to have you as a sinner. Madonna or whore—nothing in between. Why can't you ever settle for an ordinary day to day life?

You know, watching *your* fervor was as close as I ever came to religious experience. I was glad to go with you to mass every morning back then, in 1945. With you and Doria, my two big sisters, whom I had seen so little, who had been in the war.

I shivered happily in the cold church and hoped it was the beginning of ecstasy. Listened to the bells, their falling weight. Stared at the paintings and statues, watched the priest in his chasuble, but watched especially you two. The stillness and expectancy that came over you both as you knelt there. As if your near-coma could tip the scales on the side of good and hold it there while evil was throwing its weight into the balance of the quantitative battle. Any distraction would add to the unhappy teeter-totter. Were you, Andrea, already preparing to become a quantity, and quantity only, on the side of "good?" I watched you with a fervent desire to be with you, to share your spiritual adventures. Tried to participate by sheer force of concentration. I courted your passion in the belief that I was courting God. Hung out my heart where the Holy Ghost would not come to roost.

Yet even then my sympathy was with the dragon rather than with St. George. The beautiful, wild beast that twists and fights with the whole curve of its being and whose eyes burn with the fierce spring of nature rather than with a misty tangent on the infinite. While St. George stood there demurely, safe in his armor. Held a lance daintily in his right hand which seemed more used to smoothing out his curls than to forming a fist. It was clear he was not doing a thing. The action was elsewhere.

I recognized him. He performed. As I performed. In the confessional, for instance. Tried to be interesting to the priest, to make a good show of it! I perform better now. Though I still watch myself most of the time. And watch mother watch me. It gets in the way. Keeps me from letting go, being startled out of myself so that the music can take off into a space of its own, shot through to the last crevice with sound which alone moves, all by itself, penetrating, transparent, emptying me of myself. It happens, but not all the time.

SORRY.

I had to get off father. I am getting afraid of coming to believe in my theories. Of wanting to. While I play with the elements, while I put them down on paper so that they balance, if only for a moment—they

125

might begin to stick together in my mind forever, might be stronger, by sheer weight of ink, than all the other possibilities that are only thought about. The pen is a knife, and it is only in my dream that there is no one to point it at.

But I will get back to the story. With something I know.

We are into 1933. After the deal, after the Reichstag fire, after the "emergency and enabling laws," after the arrest of the communists, after the ceremony of Hitler and Hindenburg shaking hands over the tomb of Frederick the Great. After the torchlight processions, after Furtwängler's *Meistersinger* (brilliant performance, said the papers), toward the end of the school year.

"The Jews and Marxists are getting sacked."

"The teachers?"

"All branches of the civil service. Police. Post office. Etc. 'Enemies of the state cannot be employees of the state,' something like that."

"Makes sense, actually. But how do they know who's a Marxist?"

"Whoever hasn't joined the party."

FRANZ HUBER DID NOT GO QUIETLY.

A newspaper clipping. End of the school year. The students freshly washed and combed and in their Sunday best. Faces stunned from the relentless repetition of school, play, sleep. Solemn. From the mere fact of orderly assembly, each grade a little block facing the stage. Solemn by dint of reflecting the solemn platitudes addressed each year to the graduating class: *non scholae sed vitae*, not for school, it's for life that we learn. A few parents weep in the back, sensing perhaps that these kids were going out to lives as grey as their own, or even that the whole ceremony was a gathering of insects who wouldn't live to see the next dawn. But if they had thoughts like these they kept them to themselves. They would not have been popular now that the Germans had overcome the decadent defeatism of the Republic, the *Systemzeit*, now that they were refashioning a glorious nation of pure-blooded minds in pure-blooded bodies.

It was in the last, most moving minutes when all the right arms were raised at angles between 30 and 45 degrees and Germany was exalted above all other countries to Haydn's beautiful tune. The rivers that border it had been invoked (nobody minded that the text was old, out of date, that the Etsch, for instance, couldn't be called a border by any stretch of even the German imagination). There, at the last "Deutschland, Doy-oytschland," the orchestra gave out a confused cacophony. Consternation among the woodwinds. The conductor frantically waved his arms in the suddenly empty air. A single, brave violin continues a thin thread, but the assembly, jolted, confused, without strong direction, half fell silent, half finished the anthem uncertainly, each voice at its own discretion. There are instances when individualism is not desirable. Scandal. Investigations. Tearful flutists. Cowed clarinettist. Their music is found to skip a measure. *"Judenschwein* Huber" had intentionally miscopied the parts—and skipped town if he had any sense. Let's hope he still had his knack of departure. Otherwise he may not even have gotten to a concentration camp. The local SA could be trusted to take care of people like him.

A newspaper clipping. No underlining in red. No trace of mother's bow-tie mark either. Which of them had cut it out?

Did this turn mother against music? I don't think so. That came later. When she realized I was spending all my time at it and getting good. When I was to play the Mozart concerto with the school orchestra. I'd sit down to practice and:

"Lu, run and get some eggs."

"Lu, have you swept the stairs?"

"Lu, the dishes are waiting."

"Lu, post this letter right away, it's urgent."

"Lu, Frau Englert needs this."

All the while telling everybody: "My daughter Lucy is going to be the soloist at the graduation concert."

Proudly. As she later said to the neighbors:

"Bob, our American, is a professor. And my daughter Lucy studies music. Piano, yes."

Just as she used to say:

"My daughter Doria is expecting again." And: "My son-in-law has been promoted to superintendent of schools."

As she never once said to anyone:

"My daughter Andrea is in a convent."

Mother. Rigid. In the middle of the kitchen. Digging a fork into her palm. That soft palm. Her brows contracted so forcefully they seemed to cut the face in half. Not a muscle moved. Not in her face. Nor in mine where a cry suddenly had no air to sound in.

YET AT THIS TIME,

the time of the story, back in the thirties, a melody could still take hold of her. Note by note her body was shot through with music. A structure that moved with the modulating keys. A space. A space of her own. Notes toward the horizon. Against boredom. Against the kitchen window which would frame her with the scrubbed skillet or soften her outline in the steam of monday's laundry. A song. Mercury, changing so fast. Children on swings, jumping and running on and on, or slow, shadowy silk. *Lascia mi piangere.* A note held as long as possible. Till father comes in the door with "Red sky at night, sailor's delight, especially if you'd stop this screeching."

HOLD ON, ANDREA, I HAVE MORE DOCUMENTS.

A registered letter from *Kreisleiter* Müller. A summons, rather. Copies of letters Josef wrote. A scene with Müller I remember by my terror though, at the time, I didn't know what it was about. And there is my Latin teacher, Professor Acker, who was arrested by the Nazis. Little islands. If I join them all it makes a plot. But should they be joined? The real story is the water washing around them. And can I get any closer to it if I make myself immobile, without ideas or point of view? So that I disappear into that element of the story which is me: Lucy Seifert, the third daughter. Still unborn at this point. Born in 1936, the year the sea came into Providence high as a wall, tumbled into downtown all the way over to Washington Street.

BUT, OF COURSE, I WAS NOT BORN HERE, IN PROVIDENCE,

but in Kitzingen am Main where father, upright in the saddle, rode his bicycle past St. Kilian's fountain to school where, as he entered the teachers' lounge, his attention was caught by:

"This is hardly a proper comparison."

And another voice, higher, rather metallic, Fräulein Voss's:

"Not a proper comparison at all. Have you no respect for the people?"

November 1933. The results of the plebiscite. 40 million coats with white 'yes'-buttons. Damp winter coats in the foggy air. White buttons. Noticeable even in the dark, on anonymous shapes. Like patches of snow. Professor Acker had been telling of crossing the Channel to England:

"We were sitting on deck waiting for lunch. Beautiful day, marvelous blue sky. Feeling fine. At the other end of the row, a woman rushes to the railing. Throws up. The man next to her follows. Then a child. Another woman, hands clasped over her mouth. Deckchair after deckchair. The impulse skips nobody. At my end, smiles, mocking. Then the smiles fade, up and to the railing. I said to myself: this isn't going to happen to me. I feel fine. I am looking forward to lunch. I am trained in objectivity and can see the effect of mass suggestion. I have will power to resist—and then it was my turn and I was forced to the railing like everybody else."

Here he was told that his story was not a proper fable for the plebiscite. Josef turned to his colleagues:

"I used my pendulum last night, on the plebiscite. It came within 5% of the result."

Laughs. And a sudden silence. Meyer leaned forward.

"Seifert, are you making fun of the plebiscite too?"

"Not at all. I worked the pendulum on all the elections last year. Took posters home to see what kind of aura they had. You know, from the feelings of people walking by. Positive or negative charges. Only it's hard to sort this out from the charge of intention. And I hadn't tried a percentage chart before this one."

"Sancta simplicitas," mumbled Meyer.

Now here is another posssibility: Josef joined the party because the pendulum told him to. The voice from the sky, from the deep. A hazy turn towards an altitude where the bi-plane is a UFO and syntax degenerates into mountain sickness or oxygen mask while the "miraculous concatenation of logic and happiness" gets trapped in a convectional exchange and drops down between the cumulus.

VOICES. ALWAYS VOICES.

A fifth higher than Josef was comfortable with. And in his own house. He paused, his key in his hand. Why did Frederika have to have these rehearsals here, in his home. There she goes, coaching:

"Very nice. Only, don't force as you go up. Think of the handkerchief that Pippin's daughter drops. A lace handkerchief. That light."

Damn that pageant. What did Josef care how Kitzingen was founded. He wanted to be able to sit in his study and smoke a pipe. "Can't you stop this screeching," he thought. But he couldn't say it with those other women around. His ears hurt with the high notes, with the vibrato a bit too fast. Even with the door between, his ears hurt. What could he do. The sky was a dark Prussian blue. It would start raining any minute. He would drink a beer in the Würzburger Hof and hope the rehearsal will be over when he tries his door again.

Lots of people there, in the bar. Crowded. Neumann and Peters from school, Urban, Helwig and his wife, Hiesiger of the paper, lawyer Jager. And *Kreisleiter* Müller with his gang. Sure enough, "the leader says," "Jewish-Asiatic Bolshevism," "fanatic devotion," "Jewish-capitalist exploiters" shot back and forth across the table like ping pong balls. More like stones, actually, or bullets.

"Old Porzel had a heart attack. Tuesday. I saw them putting him in the ambulance."

"No wonder. I saw his girl with a Jew boy."

Müller expanded on German honor. Loud, so they can hear it over at the other tables. Racial purity. Loud, as those phrases demand to be said. From the chest, the manly German chest.

Josef nodded vaguely and steered toward a table in the corner.

"Hey, *Genosse* Seifert, there's room over here."

Some had started singing. *Die alten Germanen, die sassen...* Müller had a hard time getting his audience back. When he had a story. About Hogner. The office supply store on the Marktplatz. Hadn't registered his Jewish wife. Thought he'd get away with it because she wasn't from around here. From Graudenz. Graudenz. What a suspect place that is. Mostly Poles up there. So *Genosse* Heinlein did a checkup. Did we take Hogner by the ears! Pretended he didn't know."

Somebody started the songs up again. *Kein schöner Land...* Somebody shouted: *Heil Hitler*. The waiter closed the windows. It was getting late.

JOSEF STAYED UP LATE THAT NIGHT.

Tapped his finger against the barometer. It was falling. Stood at the window. Looked out at where the Schwanberg was, a thickening in the grey sky, maybe only because he knew it was there. Josef thought of home, of the farm, where the fog would be rising from the fields and become a great white estuary, deeper and deeper as the night advanced. Where the brook would come along, so clear you could see every pebble, every grain of sand moving in the bed.

Clear. Not like this.

Josef was worried. You, the twins, were in school. So far so good.

The wind was up from the river. Wotan's breath. It was blowing the cabbage smell out of the town toward the potato fields where you and Doria had been gathering the yellow-striped bugs all day. Better occupation than the time, a few years later, when your class went to the *Judenschule* at recess time and threw rocks. God, I can see you up there, on the bridge, right above the playground, pelting stones down at the Jewish kids, at the windows.

Memory is meant to fade, but Josef renewed its color faithfully. As the guide at Eisenach freshens the spot on the wall where Luther threw his inkwell at the devil. Quietly, slowly Josef pressed the key again to keep the string vibrating. He went in to look at Doria and you. Scrutinized your sleeping faces for likeness, racial characteristics and fear of the dark. Found only the latter which, luckily, was the one he knew how to battle. With frogs that promise to sing like nightingales. With the otter who sets his daughter on gravel near swift water. All for the sake of rhyme. With a Swahili moustache hair floating in the Kattegat. This last poem stopped him suddenly. Why would a Swahili moustache hair float in the waters of the Kattegat? Ominous. As ominous as Müllers's hand on his shoulder.

"Why don't you ever stop by the office, *Genosse*. Would like to chat with you some time."

Josef was worried. Worried enough to write a letter withdrawing his appeal of verdict AW/I/564c dated February 18, 1933 which upheld decision JH/III/3864b of January 30, 1930.

"...in these times of national regeneration...all energies must serve the state...The large goals...supersede private quarrels..."

Got the jargon down pretty fast. And ended, as it was getting light, in the required fashion. A dry staccato. With German greetings. *Mit deutschem Gruss: Heil Hitler.* Did he have visions of you and Doria being kicked out of the public school and made to go the the *Judenschul*? Getting stones thrown at you instead of throwing them? He would rather see you marching in rows of three, in blue skirts and white blouses, shouldering spades. *Arbeitsdienst.* Service to the country.

"Are you willing to make the earth fertile?"

"We are."

An army of teenage girls. For *Führer* and fatherland.

Did Josef imagine you wearing the yellow star on your coats and advertising Frederika's infidelity to the world? Kitzingen? The world?

His honor. His honor?

AWOKE FROM THE ACHE IN HIS NECK.

Strained muscles. His eyes opened out on green and white, black spots, lines. Every particle intruded on his retina on its own terms, separately. Gradually his eyes focused on "Heil Hitler," the letter, the stained green blotter which covered a third of his desk, the piles of books open and closed, with bits of paper stuck in, passages under-lined, annotated, questioned. His blood beat through his temples with a thump like the anvil in *Siegfried.*

The dream. Yes, the dream. Still piercing his brain as with a sharp beak.

He is climbing a mountain. Maybe the Schwanberg. Steeper. Stonier. Oberhausenstein, then. Yes, down below, the familiar roofs of the sheds, the stables, the silo. He is trying to rush up into the air. Fighting gravity. Mineral deposits glisten between juniper and pine. Long narrow veins, they gather the pale light into threads up the white stone. Up, way up with the clouds, Frederika. She waves. Calls out to assure him he will never make it. Never in the world. He throws off ballast: his watch, his knife. Frederika flushed, a cold fire in her eyes, sings the definite articles: der die das, der die das.

He tries to hold on to pieces of moss, small branches of juniper, painfully, they scratch his face.

"Frederika," he cries. "There is no way."

She sings: Kiss my ass, kiss my ass.

Underbrush gives way to rock. Bone-white and sheer in the moon. And suddenly the twins on his shoulders, romping. Giddyup. The last branch gives. A voice like a hawk's swoops through the air. By the ears. The rushing air. The jerking pain. He is being held: by the ears. Sharp beaks tear his lobes. Wings, he thinks, wings. And tries to shake the twins off. His ears tear. He falls as fast as his blood.

Josef massaged his neck. The dream had gone back where it came from. To be replayed. With a new twist perhaps, new props. By the same actors, always. At the next curtain of sleep.

Presently the apartment would fill with the morning clatter. Frederika cross. But there would be coffee. The air rang with the twins' quarrels over the bathroom. Steps seemed to eat up space, shrink it. Too many for the little corridor. Clatter of pots. Pulse of the day, the effort of waking. He put his hand on the crystal paperweight heavy enough to resist his touch, to affirm coolly its roundness, its reality. He stretched and walked over to the barometer. Tapped it lightly with his finger. The needle quivered, but stayed where it was: falling.

"So this is where you are."

Frederika. Her head through the door. Hands behind her back tying her apron.

"Drunk last night?"

FEAR

has as many shades as experience. Its punctuation is varied, its reflexes broken. Fluttering nerves. Notes frantically scattered. Explosion or closing in. A ghostly flitting ride on a dotted 6/8 rhythm which finally sinks to the uncanny depth of a pianissimo bass. Doppelgänger or lacking shadow, vagina dentata or thunder and lightning. Shadow cast by a foetus. The curve of a nose.

Josef went to the bathroom and combed his hair back to his old "popo part." The question was: had Müller been drunk enough that one could ignore his "invitation?" Was it safer to stay away or to ingratiate himself? Josef tried the pendulum. But the oracle refused to commit itself. Said yes on the first try, no on the second, stayed on the platform of the present and refused to roll its circles into any muddy future. He opened a book at random and hit on "It is dangerous to bury people too soon, even though the body may show undoubted signs of putrefaction."

On this advice, for which he thanked Mme. Blavatsky, he decided to lie low.

He went for long walks, beyond the outskirts of town. Down the river. Sandy paths. Apple trees with cracked bark. He walked and he stood still. The water muddy with the fall rains. Muddy like doubt.

Kreisleiter Müller, *Kreisleiter* Müller, cried the sparrows and veered away from the glittering aluminum scarecrows in the vinyards which were turning the lightest bit red already. Josef looked at the line they traced in the sky. If only we could read. Surrounded by signs. If only we had the key. Or somebody to talk to about all this. These German matters. Jewish matters. The twins. How accessible were those files. The Ministry of Education. Peaceful coexistence. Why did it not seem possible? Among decent people. Decent people?

BLOOD,

they say. Blood tells. Blood is cordial. *Ein ganz besondrer Saft.* Good to sign pacts with. The purity of blood. And no test to tell him if the blood in these children is his or Franz's, Aryan or Jewish. Blood does not distinguish. Not type A at any rate. And they don't look Jewish. Blood. It is as blind as the mole it is, burrowing through its veins and arteries. Blood is for fools and thicker than water. You try to fish in blood and you fish yourself trouble. They would do well to remember this, the blood and soil fellows. There is many a fish in the sea and but four kinds of blood. He had read books on genetics, on blood types. Hoping for clues, for certainty. Landsteiner and Levine. Von Dungern, Hirzfeld, Bernstein. Jewish names, half of them. No wonder they came up with co-dominants. Co-dominant A and B. Co-dominant alleles. O is recessive. Antigens and antibodies. Phenotypes and genotypes. Jews. From co-dominant to recessive. O. Zero.

"Saw Seifert wandering around last night. Said hello, but he looked straight through me."

"Probably took you for ectoplasm. Or, what's the other thing he talks about? Effluvia."

"Crazy fellow."

134

A storm uprooted an oak on Moltkestrasse. Wotan's tree. A sign? The moon very clear, very white with a forecasting of frost. Already. Its light filled the street except for an occasional shadow. *Kreisleiter* Müller drunk or sober. Does he remember or does he not. What does he want and what does he know. From the park by St. Kilian's fountain came a noseful of rotting apple and mixed with the smell of recent rain.

But the day comes up every day. Grey and white. With fog from the river. Cut into strips by the noise of the magpies.

And Frederika's refrain:

"Had a good time with your mistress?"

Josef's muscles contracted. He pretended not to hear. Then it rained again.

"God, she doesn't even have a place to take you out of the rain?" Frederika slammed the muddy shoes into the sink. "A two-bit upright. And then I'm good enough to clean his majesty's boots."

The syllabus had been revised. Staff and student body changed. *Aufgenordet.* Purged of its Arons and Cohens and Goldschmidts and Blumenfelds and of less obvious names. Acker did not talk about England much anymore. Not even about the Elgin marbles.

Perhaps Josef had been forgotten. Go underground. Part your hair in the middle. Avoid bars. Avoid the street of the party office. Protective coloring. Background features. Body longing to be flat with the ground.

THEN A GUST

like a wind from the East, driving the river before it. Down the valley, no Schwanberg in its way to break it. Like a storm whipping up waves enough to sink the sluggish barges filled to the brim with sand — a thing which does not happen often here in mild Franconia or they would not glide as calmly as in a water color by Dietrich Bennig.

A summons: *Genosse* Seifert to report at the NSDAP office on Monday, July 16, 1939. Registered letter.

"*Genosse* Seifert. Been a long time. Not very eager to see us."

"I've been very..."

"Very passive, yes. That's what you meant to say, wasn't it. I don't think I even saw you at the 9th-of-November celebration. That's quite a while back, but we have good memories here. Very good memories."

Müller paused. Looked at the tip of his cigarette. Josef mumbled about lots of work.

"Work. Precisely what I want to talk about. I hope you realize that the work of prime importance is the spiritual renewal of our nation. I don't underrate the work you do in the schools. On the contrary: the youth of the country is in your hands. I hope you realize your responsibility. How important it is that the teachers should have the right attitudes. We did the groundwork, getting rid of the destructive foreign element that infested the system. But it's not enough."

He paused to put out his cigarette and light another. His eyes on its tip, he went on:

"We need reliable people in the schools. People who make sure our children are not exposed to Jewish-internationalist corrosion. Let's be honest —" he gave Josef a practiced piercing look, "even pure Aryan blood is no guarantee against a perverse brain. We've had reports."

Josef's neck was getting warm. His pulse coded danger.

Another pause.

"Reports from parents. From students. From our research staff. Concerning political records, concerning remarks in the classroom, concerning past contacts with yids, concerning sexual mores, concerning..."

Did Josef only imagine that Müller looked sharply at him at items three and four? Saliva shot into his mouth. He swallowed. His tongue seemed to float in a pool he tried to drain against the roof of his mouth and swallow again. Hold on, he told himself. Don't defend yourself before you're accused. Did Josef only imagine that Müller droned on about past mistakes, possibility to make good, to prove one's loyalty? He could not be sure because he listened for clues to what Müller knew. What and how much of it. This research staff, was it a bluff? He came to, abruptly, on Müller's:

"Do you follow me?"

What did Josef reply? Shall we play again, Andrea?

AT MULTIPLE CHOICE, THIS TIME?

NUMBER ONE: Josef rose slowly.

"Are you suggesting I become an informer? A spy? And against Acker in particular?"

136

And when Müller sneered: "Delighted to hear you put it in such precise terms. I tip my hat to the Germanist," Josef turned on his heels to leave.

Then?

Müller smiled: "Don't be in such a rush, *Genosse*. *Genosse* Helwig wants to talk to you too."

Continuation of persuasion by other means.

Or perhaps he only threatened: "*Genosse* Seifert. Haven't you forgotten something?"

Josef stopped in his tracks.

"We salute before we leave. *And* be sure to give my very special regards to your very lovely wife. I shall be seeing both of you very soon. I am looking forward to it very much. Heil Hitler."

NUMBER TWO: The Balancing Act.

"Father, what's that pole for you're carrying up on the tightrope?"

"Balance. That's what I hold on to."

"I thought you didn't hold on to anything."

"If I don't hold on to something I'll fall."

"But what if the pole falls?"

"Blockhead. How can it fall: I'm holding it."

NUMBER THREE: The saving of the skin. He takes up the scent. Blood. Its rapacity.

What is your guess, Andrea? I have little hope for the heroic. And I pray that he was not willing to cooperate. No, I am sure, he could not have been. I would put my money on number two. The innocent as a dove and wise as a serpent middle path. Trying to wriggle through. Pretending to cooperate and playing for time. Do you think he tried to warn Acker? Or was he afraid to: Acker might be a test case, might be there to report on Seifert? Did he put a little special emphasis in his words when he answered an Ackerism with:

"You can't mean this. No true German can think so. You're just testing us."

And the menace: "I trust you will wash your ears." Did Josef hold out? Could he hold out? Did this interview take place? In any form? Something took place.

SEPTEMBER 1, 1939.

I am sitting on father's lap with my doll Ulli. In father's study. We are sitting, mother opposite, by the little round wicker table. The table with the radio on it. War. The renewed Polish provocation was more than "the boiling soul of the German people" could take. *Die kochende Volksseele.* I remember mother's disdainful: "War! It'll be over in four weeks. Our leader will take care of it." And father right down to the recruiting office.

He is beyond drafting age.

He pleads special training.

It is out of date.

Not so. Josef has kept up with the flying courses and *Fachzeitschriften.* He might qualify as an aviation instructor. His case will be considered.

AIRFIELDS

were being built all over. Josef was made flying instructor with the rank of captain at Flugplatz Kitzingen. No more knickerbockers and socks on suspenders. A field grey coat swishing open over high leather boots. No more seeing Acker. But Kitzingen: still in Müller's district. And home to Frederika in the evening. Home to the fighting, the constant chafing, the venom breaking out, the fury. Frederika had reason to fret:

"I thought it would all be over in a couple of weeks. Polacks. I know about them. There were plenty of them around Berlin. Pack of dumb and lazy good-for-nothings. But dragging on like this. Ration cards. And that awful Frau Hasse. Acts as if she were the Führer in person."

"I hope you're polite with her. She's the block warden. Don't attract attention."

"Of course I'm polite. Who's talking! But you should hear her brag about husband and four sons at the front."

"Alright. I'm trying to get there too."

"That's not my idea."

It was *father's* idea. He wrote letters again. Requested to be put on active duty. Pleaded experience and overview as the mature man's assets. As good as, or in the case of air warfare, better than mere youth.

THE HAWTHORN WAS IN BLOOM.

Thick strings of blossoms, little red balls burst through the foliage. I took up my spring occupation: digging little holes into the stucco of the house, down to the brick. Behind the house was Kummor's printshop. OFFSET LETTERPRESS LITHOGRAPHY. The yard was littered with square slabs of stone still showing the wine labels printed from them. IPHÖFER KRONSBERG. ESCHERNDORFER LUMP. RÖDELSEER KÜCHENMEISTER. WÜRZBURGER STEIN.

One label made me wonder: WITTLINGER SCHLAN-GENGRABEN. Wine from the snakepit? Interwoven letters, a coat of arms and two smiling boys on either side—just heads and hands. Postures like you and Doria at Mespelbrunn. Postures like Raphael's putti. Father should have pasted this label under the photo also.

BUT HERE CAME ELEGANT HERR SCHADERER

with his walking stick tapping its metal point against the pavement. Tap and two and three and tap and two and three. It was dinner and cards. Dr. Knottinger arrived at the same moment and the two men talked all the way up the staircase. Upstairs there was Frederika all in a flurry and Beppo, take their coats, will you, and O the beautiful flowers, how delightful, are they from your garden? And Fräulein Voss. But the younger men are not there. Not Vogel. Not Schuster. Not Meyer. Herr Schaderer stood with Josef by the coatrack.

"Acker?"

"The grumpy fellow?" This is Frederika. "What about him?"

"Arrested. This morning."

Schaderer put his hat back on. He had been switching it from one hand to the other waiting for Josef to take it.

"Why?"

Schaderer shrugged.

"Who? Acker?" Fräulein Voss's question as they went into the dining room where the table was already set. No splendor of aspic in the center, though. Not now. Not with rations.

"Acker had it coming. Never could keep his mouth shut."

"The things he said even in the street."

"I sometimes thought he must be an agent. Trying to trap us into saying the same sort of thing. There are spies on the staff."

Josef wondered: Do they know? Are they testing me? Have we all been to see Müller? But he said:

"They don't need spies on the staff to arrest us."

Said it so vehemently that Fräulein Voss raised her eyebrows:

"Now, now, Josef. We live in a *Rechtsstaat*. We'll find out about it all at the trial."

Frederika came carrying the steaming soup bowl. Herr Englert behind her.

"For heaven's sake, still standing!"

Twists and turns and shuffling of chairs and a sigh from arthritic Bennig.

"What's this about a trial?"

"Acker's been arrested."

Englert filled his glass and let it run over. He looked frightened. The soup was eaten a bit quietly. But it was eaten. Couldn't afford to skip a meal even if the news went to the stomach.

PROFESSOR ACKER KNEW

or thought he knew why he was arrested, sent to a camp, then transferred to the army in 1941. He talked about it. In 1946. When he taught Latin again.

"Not that I did anything heroic. But I owned a house. A very nice house. Herr Müller thought so too. The *Kreisleiter*. *Sella in curulis*. I didn't have the decency to be Jewish or at least have a Jewish wife to make it easy for them to confiscate it. Had to work a little harder, the bastards, the *irrumatores*."

We held our breath. I would have drawn it in more sharply yet if I had dreamed of any possible connection with father. But Acker did not seem to think so. I hold on to his version with all my might.

"Damn little you needed to say to be a traitor. Attentive students, I must say. They had listened. Could repeat it back to me verbatim. And don't you feel superior. You'd do the same thing. They thought they were doing their duty. Saving the fatherland from bolshevist-capitalist corrosion."

He shot us a quick look to see if we took that in. From eyes sheltered under bushy grey brows. He did not like the light. Kept the blinds down always. Hard to imagine him in a Roman day where the sun stays and chisels its date into the stone, reversing the direction of even the flightiest time. His hair, grey, did not take the light either, did not let it play. We grinned our appreciation which brought a sarcastic smile in reply.

"Don't think I made that up. There's no discrimination in hatred. *"nam nihil est quicquam sceleris, quo prodebat ultra. non si demisso se pise uoret capite.*

"Again, please, Fräulein Weber, and watch your vowels. They are impure—halfway between dialect and corset when they should come straight from the vulva. Go ahead. You can do it. If your Latin is good enough you can get me into jail again. Brand new Christian Democratic jail. Still takes damn little. Different things, of course."

COINCIDENCES.

Co-incidences. Falling with, falling at the same time, falling into place. Gravity. Like Schumann's op. 17, which wants to be a Beethoven sonata, but the thematic figures have too much weight of their own to fuse into a stringent process. Instead of development: encounter.

Maybe wanting to make sense of it is to make sure of missing it. If I point a knife at a person he is likely to run. A given hammer speed can only produce a certain loudness of tone. But wait, Andrea, now we finally get to something I witnessed.

AN EARLY SUMMER SUNDAY IN 1941.

Father was to leave for the front in a week. The letters had finally worked. Also, the drafting age was going up. We were taking our last Sunday walk. A breath of fresh air, a look around "god's beautiful handiwork." We. Josef, Frederika and I. Where were you, Andrea? You and Doria? *Arbeitsdienst* I suppose. Or were you still too young to wield a spade? Summer camp of the BDM then. *Bund deutscher Mädel.* Pretty brisk too. Navy blue skirts and white blouses. Ties, with a braided leather knot to slip them through. Which gets taken away if you are late for the meetings. Breaking the rules. Shame. Unworthy of the leather. The brown leather. Campfires and gathering potato bugs. First aid and marches through town.

At any rate, you are not of the party. An ordinary walk. With an occasional good afternoon Herr Professor, Heil Hitler and any news from your husband? At the edge of the woods, café Waldesruh. Not as quiet as its name would have us believe. The garden tables are crowded. Noisy. Jolly people, the Kitzingers. Tall white coffee pots. Beerglasses with a filigree of foam dried on the glass. Half Kitzingen is recovering from the effort of their Sunday walk. Those who came out here by car look cooler and down on the others. The coffee is already ersatz. *Malzkaffee.* But you still can get cake if you sacrifice a couple of squares of your ration card. No cream, of course. The radio announced that this speech was being broadcast by the *Deutschlandsender* in conjunction with the radios of the protectorates Holland, Norway, Greece, Luxembourg, France, Serbia, and the allied states of Italy, Hungary, Roumania. Talk of *Blitzkrieg* and is it hot enough for you and Hitler knows what he's doing. Talk of the organization is fabulous and of invading England. *Und wir fahren gegen Engel-land.* Also talk of Russia and *Zweifrontenkrieg.* With a trace of worry. Two-front-war.

Frau Kupferberg got us a table inside. After all, we were regulars. Every Sunday afternoon. "Lovely day today, isn't it. And the war will be over any time now." The beer she pushed across the tables left a wet trail.

At another table, uniforms. "Field grey" soldiers on leave and older brown shirts with their broad leather belts. *Kreisleiter* Müller presides. Stories from the front. Hands diving through the air. Planes? Bombs? Grenades? Crash and explosions. And: "We on the home front." Frau Kupferberg was excited. Hovered around their table. Noise. Shouting. Jovial, it seemed. Suddenly father, upright:

"Herr Kreisleiter, will you step outside with me."

Sudden silence. Müller got up slowly, glared at father. Frau Kupferberg stopped frozen in her tracks, then rushed to turn up the radio. *Prinz Eugen, der edle Ritter* boomed the velvety basses. Müller let out a laugh:

"Na dann los, Leute."

FATHER WITH A BLOODY FACE.

Hurried us out. Past the stares in the garden. The late afternoon sun was heavy, the colors dusty. We had trudged a ways when a car stopped.

142

"I'm Dr. Wunderlich. Get in." And a bit later: "What was it about?"

"Personal," said father, cautious. "Somebody insulted my wife."

"The somebody was obvious enough. You'll forgive my waiting a few minutes. Too old to take chances."

"Aren't you taking chances anyway?"

"*Ach was.* Professional ethic."

At home, father's nose properly swabbed and bandaged, we were packing while his eye turned purple.

"Now who was preaching about lying low? Playing the hero! Attacking a bully like that. And then you can't admit you got beaten. Strategy indeed."

"Not the eiderdown. Are you crazy? On the bicycle?"

Only a few things. Only for a few days. Till father leaves for the front.

"Why *did* you challenge him?"

"Did you want me to accept the "Jew whore" he threw at you? Do you know what that would mean?"

"Can't protest except with your fists. Men!"

"It's *his* language. And you think I'd be dumb enough not to let him win? My nose may save us a very unpleasant visit."

"Then why do we have to leave and hide?"

"Dr. Wunderlich doesn't take chances either."

"Fine man that, I must say. Elegant too. But where does the money come from, suddenly, to stay at Frau Wittig's? You said we couldn't take even a weekend's vacation."

"Will you please hurry up?"

"Or don't you have to pay her? Is she one of your whores?"

"At least she's not a Jew whore."

THE BICYCLES

rolled downstream, toward Marktbreit. Evening came with pale colors and quiet up from the water. Calmed Josef and Frederika. Perhaps they just needed all their breath for pedaling. High in my saddle behind father's handlebars I must have seen farther West than usual. The horizon is a function of the eye level. The Main stroked in and out of the fields, the tongues of woods. Soft, swelling sandbanks and burned-up grass. Along the road, rows of plumtrees that would soon give up their purple load to be turned into Schnapps. On toward the thin, tapered roof of the steeple, so steep that your eyes slip down the blue slate, right to Frau Wittig's door.

Provisional states have their own pleasure, like the hour before a battle, the space of approach. I woke early. It was hot under the blankets. I didn't have my own bed. I wriggled out from between mother and father. A few days. Mother helped in the kitchen. Tense. Father came and went. Tense.

Then the bicycles rode back to Kitzingen. Then to the train station. Father tried to get the window of his compartment down, pulling and shaking. His face got red. Little beads of sweat appeared.

"Don't bother, Beppo, leave it alone."

But he got it down just as the whistle shrilled, long enough to lean out and say:

"Be good. Don't give mother any trouble."

Mother stuck a handkerchief in my hand:

"Wave."

Not an impressive train. No crowds with flowers, waving, no Red Cross women in their blue and white stripes handing coffee and sandwiches to the soldiers. No festive atmosphere. Nor when he came back. Minus a leg. Plus an Iron Cross First Class. In 1942. In time for other bicycle flights, from the firebombs, when I rode my own. What if we should be buried in those heavy cellars smelling of wine. Like the Kochs and Jägers, the Kleins and Havermanns and Schulzes. Anything rather than that. Rather catch it in the open and a quick death. Rather jump on bicycles with the first note of the siren and be out in the road. Flat in the ditches as the planes came roaring. The frightful planes. Explosions. Fire somehere. And to see it all rather than bury my face in a heap of potatoes and feel the ground shaking. Simply ran and pedaled off, father and mother and I. Father with a little sling over his right pedal. His good leg on double duty, pushing down and pulling up. He came also in time for the Corpus Christi procession.

THE PROCESSION.

My first. One of a dozen little girls dolled up in our Sunday best, nervous about how fast to strew our flowers. Father Ramberg gathered the schoolchildren around him.

"It is part of your courage in demonstrating your faith that you will not react in any way if there should be taunts from the bystanders."

We did not feel the least bit like the early Christians he invoked. Giggly, rather, because Hans pulled Erna's braid, and she turned so fast she spilled half her flower basket. But then the blue robe of the madonna rose on the first notes from the glinting brass, rose up into the blue of the sky. Only a little ways, though, then hovered, hesitant, wavering just above our heads and allowed herself to be absorbed into the narrow Kirchgasse.

Steps that took possession, but hesitantly. Steps that marked out the town as God's, the Catholic God's. Only, it was not much of the town. We crept along the Main River from the parish church to the convent of St. Ursula. Narrow streets. Narrow old houses, close together. Up the hill to St. Francis' chapel, neatly avoiding the burned Synagogue by one block. Then back down to the river. "The Presence" barely edged the south and west of Kitzingen.

In 1946, when you came home, Andrea, the route changed. Back to what it had been before 1933. It went downtown. An altar smack on the townhall steps, right opposite St. Kilian's fountain. He of Wotan's oak. There were policemen to stop the traffic. Whenever there was a measure of rest in the hymn you could hear the back end of the caterpillar dragging its notes after—so large was the procession. And the feet marked the route with obvious assurance, steps in full possession, steps that would walk this way again and again.

Not like the measly bunch of 1942. A few schoolchildren, nuns, some women, old people screeching the hymns in wavering voices. Very few men. Father, yes. With his hair parted in the middle, though this was perhaps the one day when he should have combed it into his forehead. His little moment of courage, of perfectly pointless courage. Father with his cane and wooden leg. With his decoration. What about not attracting attention?

"They'll get you," said mother. "When you don't even believe."

"What do you know what I believe."

"I know they take pictures."

Maybe they did. Nothing else happened that I could see. Calm, anticyclonic conditions. Maybe the brownshirts had been out in earlier years. In 1942, the lack of scoffers was disappointing. When I had braced myself for an arena full of lions!

Still, except for father's stubborn wooden stomping, we all expected the ground to give way to an emptiness which I could not picture any more than God, yet which we approached as certainly as the believer approaches this unimaginable "Presence" in the little white wafer, floating on whatever deal the priest had made with the mayor.

THE PROCESSION, PASSING THE LEIDENHOF, THE COURT OF SUFFERING,

stepped into the void and its fall echoed down four centuries, to 1525, into cries of Here Steckelberg —Here Würzburg, Here Protestant —Here Catholic. Matters of conscience, insurrection, pieties of reading the Bible or a pilgrimage to Our Lady of Altötting, investitures, faith and works.

The Bishop of Würzburg opens his hand on the way to a blessing. A moment only, but time enough for a purse to slide into it. There is dark enough for secret messages. Cuius regio eius religio. Ruler's religion, religion of the ruled. Ten men tied, on their knees in the court, a judge and a priest in black robes, the hangman in red, assistants, a pan fire. A glowing iron. Ten screams. Ten pairs of eyes that presumed to read the Bible for themselves. The priest intones a prayer to leave the right impression with the crowd. Subdued, the crowd. Then a bustle of packing up, sand and sawdust.

Spies. Troops of landsknechts ride into town. Or an encounter in the fields. A coach near Dettelbach where the Main curves. Suddenly, a hawk's cry, short, shrill, an armed band out of the woods and another up from the bank. Negotiations. Ransom. Money. Territory.

Now Kitzingen belongs to Count Steckelberg who has the ears of the leading Catholics. Has them cut off. An eye that reads for an ear that listens to authority. Same robes. Same place. Leidenhof. Court of pain.

And shortly after, the bishop's troops and the count's side by side against the peasant bands with pitchforks and scythes, with the bundschuh tied to a pole.

"That's not what I meant at all with the freedom of a Christenmensch," cries Luther. "Strike them down, those limbs of Satan, those firebrands out of hell, throttle and stab them, they are no better than mad dogs. The ass must have his blows and the rabble must be ruled by force."

They struck them down, whether Catholic or Lutheran. Not all, though, who would work the fields? But enough. And this sculptor, one

146

of the leaders. Meister Tilman Riemenschneider whose hands could be cut off without danger to the economy. Who cared for his reliefs, gesniten auff zwey oder drey finger hoch. *The gall he had to picture a peasant mob with scythes behind Jesus riding into Jerusalem. Highly unsuitable and inaccurate.*

The Leidenhof still where it was. Still part of the prison. If I had been more aware I could have looked up to the windows for Professor Acker, for the Jews of Kitzingen, the Marxists. I would have noticed women looking up at the wall as the procession hurried past, at the small windows where there was nothing to see.

NOW I AM GETTING GARRULOUS

as if a whole lost vocabulary burst open and out of control. But you are wrong to say I paint theater backdrops. The background is real enough. It is the actors that get caught between too much and too little, and do not know how to go on. Not a proper drama where one incident follows logically, with necessity from the one before. No fugue. At best, theme and variations. Short-winded motives linked by the surging of a minor chord. Conjectures. I throw out threads, and if I were Mozart I could gather in complete ideas.

FATHER'S PENDULUM

won't help us either, even though it became the oracle of Kitzingen and environs. Father's triumph. It lasted just a little longer than the interest in his scandal, lasted while there were families without news from their soldiers, while there were people missing on the flight from the East, from the bombed cities.

One after another they came. For certainty, they said, and meant hope. Nobody snickered about superstition. Information at any price, from any source. At night, when I had gone to bed, Josef muffled himself in his coat and pored over rows of snapshots, over the unformed faces of young soldiers, the lined faces of not so young soldiers. Tried to catch the residue of aura clinging to the likeness. Tried to sort out life and death, the ellipses of breath and the immobile point. The dark is a good conductor. It circulates freely between souls. The hope of anxious wives and parents pulled at the pendulum. Josef braced himself. To be pure medium, transmitter of just enough impulse to respond to the flicker of living distress behind the pictures. He steeled himself against his sinking heart, reined in his own energy ready to roar into the act, the faint stir. He shuffled the photos like cards, turned them face down. Tried to unclench his muscles into objectivity, his role as catalyst, and hold back in his throat his own screams of love, hate and fear of death. Did he succeed when he took out Franz's photo? Did he ever take out Franz's photo?

There was a letter from some prison camp. Another belated "Fallen on the field of honor." As the pendulum had indicated. Photos of women, children, aged people joined those of the soldiers. The whole town was ringing our door bell. It seemed they were queuing up for blocks. Entire streets solid with people bore down on Josef's night while he tried to ride unknown dimensions against six one way and half a dozen the other. And found mostly death. Machine guns and exploding shells, heads striking the ground in numbers that denied the irreplaceable nature of each. Bones snapping, the signals taken back. Farther, much farther out than he had meant to go. Did the pendulum stick to the deaths on "the field of honor" or did it spell out other names, which Josef might have known if he had read the signs of the times rather than of the sky? Names which he'd rather not know, which might mark the death of Franz whom he'd rather forget? Names like Dachau, Buchenwald, Flossenburg, Mauthausen, Ravensbruck, Bergen-Belsen, Oranienburg, Neuengamme, Stutthof, Sachsenhausen, Theresienstadt, Auschwitz, Maidanek, Treblinka? The last circle of hell. Which he could not stand to look at. *If* he looked. In any case, he scrambled back, desperately: Back to a stomach that wants to vomit. To the rhythm of stump and foot. To the finger on the barometer. To the itch in the crotch. To the stable elements, adagio and senza tempo. To the fighting with Frederika.

WHICH WENT ON. AND ON.

It filled the room with secret bank accounts, with mistresses, with illegitimate children. The money must be going somewhere. Josef must be making more than the pittance of household budget and rent. And mother such a thrifty shopper.

Josef got his black look, struck at waste, at lack of planning. But mistresses and bastards attacked him from behind. Now he got up on the high horse, his one foot in the stirrup. He even put pipe and book down, indignant, to seize the reins:

"You know perfectly well that this is slander. Without the slightest foundation."

But Frederika had an attack prepared, from the flank:

"If there is no mistress, then why do you not tell me how much you actually earn? Why don't we work out the budget together?"

Now what could he say? He did not make it up onto the horse, that's for sure. He whirled the prerogative of the provider about. But already on the defensive. Already only holding his ground. But this firmly. Horse or no horse. Here they deadlocked. On the minted metal. On their hind legs. Here they honed their tongues and clenched their fists. Here their flesh would rot rather than give ground.

DAMN LONG, ANDREA.

You've taken damn long to admit that you are upset by the new father I've given you. All this bitching me up about Bob! And you still try to mask what bothers you: Josef's memory. "Say nothing but good about the dead." Whereas I always go for the worst possibilities. True. I suppose the proverb and the Carmelites are right: Silence is golden. It might have been better to wear a piece of wood over my mouth than say some of what I've said. But it is not that I want Josef to myself.

Franz Huber. The weight of a name. It pulls vague possibility down to sperm and egg. Andrea Huber? Andrea Seifert? I'm sorry to give you another identity jolt. I too prefer knowing who my father is even if I'm not happy with him. Certainty, again. It's hard to come by.

DID I TELL YOU

about the time Josef sent me after mother when she had run out one night? After the knife episode. I was thrilled to be a spy, seriously, not playing at it, but also terrified. I anticipated the moment when I would have to lunge forward and stop her. From what? From killing herself, I hoped. Anything rather than meeting a lover who might turn out to be *my* father. There had been enough digs to make me wonder.

Hands thrust into her coat pockets, she walked with short, determined steps. Not a meditative walk where the foot slowly feels its way along the possibilities of thought and sentence. She walked like an harangue, crushing each word by the force with which it was hurled.

I don't recall the weather. The sky might have been black construction paper with bits of mica for all I knew. I remember, at every street corner, my premonition of disaster. As if Frederika were a magnet drawing toward herself all the loose, still unattached catastrophes, be they lovers or drunken drivers.

I must have been ten at least, because there was no more Adolf-Hitler-Strasse or Horst-Wessel-Platz. Instead Rilkestrasse. Mother held her head high, like a first soprano in the State Opera, like a woman who knows where she is going. On past the leaning tower, past the Capitol Cinema, down to the river. I did not know what I would do if she crossed the embankment. I think I expected the moment of action to make me "real," let me grow up, live, whatever. The rubber band would hold mother on the muddy path or would take me down with her as you can take a body down into the waves of sleep.

I am sure she met a lover. But I do not remember anything beyond getting to the river. Nothing at all. Not even how I got home. I blanked it out, couldn't stand the shape of my potential father. But maybe I remembered long enough to tell Josef and then blanked it all out: lover, father *and* stool-pigeoning?

BETWEEN, ALWAYS.

Between father and mother. Between memory and conjecture. Between English with a German accent and "For an American your German is excellent." Between husband and lover. No, Bob has not come back. Nothing has happened, been resolved, decided. But I have cleaned up. A couple of days ago, a raw egg slipped out of my hand onto the floor. I ignored it. Took another egg. It also slipped. I imagined losing my gauge of strength, so that I'd always either drop or crush the egg, either my hands or my soles covered with slime. I stepped out of my clogs and stuck my toe into the eggwhite, smearing it around the dirt till I was suddenly shaking with disgust. Then worked myself into a real fury of scrubbing till I was wet all over. My shirt clung to my back by dark stains. Pants wadded in my crotch. Some substitute for sex! But the body slides out of your hold this way too.

Also, I'm working. So I've missed a few rehearsals. It feels strange, though. The notes go out and dissolve in too empty a space.

If Bob came back? If the string I've pulled tighter and tighter did not snap but suddenly slackened? Taken by surprise. Would I be? Taken? Andrea, you think of love as a fight against chance, as a possible logic chaining incidents together. With premises and conclusions. You have to realize, it is nothing but a chain of accidents itself. Maybe not even a chain. In love more than anywhere else you have to consider the open borders. More than in any other experience that you might want to tell many times, from various angles, in various sequences, but always with the same sentences, like a memory of parents.

Between the cradle and the grave. Father and mother. Holding a single note as long as possible I let, slowly, all the air out of my lungs.

What more is there to add? No resolution. A dissonant suspension with always the beginning of new motions, nervous twitch, clash of opposing tensions holding together like the stresses of a building.

JOSEF RETREATED TO HIS STUDY.

As much as possible. Possible can mean many things. For instance the weather, the winter months when only the living room was heated. Even then he often braved a cold age of Goethe or the certainly icy "higher planes" more easily than the steamy warmth where mother's voice cut with the edge of a butcher knife. It reached him anyway, though, followed him into the study with an added sharpness from the chill it had traveled through.

Finally there was no choice but to stick together, sit together, lie together. A newspaper came in handy to make a private space. Or a school book, my own horizon, shielding my eyes if not ears. Franz Huber was never mentioned. Neither was the word "Jew."

Years and years. Unsegmented like the unbarred "prose" sections in the Concord Sonata—complex, expanding, a fluttering of nerves and wind, the notes frantically scattered through progressively widening intervals.

Remarks were dropped and not picked up. They did not mean anything anyway. There was small hope that a phrase might not stay where it had fallen, but pick itself up into a bridge. Then it might stroke you all the way down to the period. But it was knives, rather, daggers and axes that were dropped here. A heap of scrap metal built up in the middle of the Seifert living room. Sentence by sentence. Grunt by frown. Easy transitions: love to hatred. Somebody ought to clear it all out. Instead, we moved away.

AND EVEN NOW

I was going to pull out and leave the heap there, in the middle of the room, to rust. I've added to it. The new blades jump into sight, shiny, stainless. They catch the sun as it goes down in the window. The knives remain. The oak stumps, the scars, the empty sockets. The reasons for striking change and are gone. Father is dead. Bob and Laff are gone. Mother sits at her window in castle Schwanberg. Old Folks Home. Maybe it is the same window where Pippin's daughter sat and dropped her hanky which I picked up and thought I could pull over all this, Franz Huber included.

But you are right not to let me. You are right to insist that I help you find out what happened to him. After all, I have given him to you, Andrea, given you his name. Franz Huber. It is not likely we'll succeed. Less likely yet that we will find him alive even if he got out on Bernstein money and for a while said "piffle paffle" in Brooklyn or Chicago. He would be well over eighty now. And in any case, we know what the odds are: Dachau, Buchenwald, Mauthausen...

874941

Waldrop, Rosmarie ~~ONE WEEK NOT RENEWABLE~~

The hanky of Pippin's

874941

Waldrop, Rosmarie

The hanky of Pippin's
daughter
~~ONE WEEK NOT RENEWABLE~~

DEC 1 0 1990 *Gebel*

9/87